302.50973
POV

A2170 647870 1

W9-CEK-389

Poverty

Other Books of Related Interest:

Opposing Viewpoints Series

Homelessness

Juvenile Crime

The Minimum Wage

Unemployment

At Issue Series

Are Women Paid Fairly?

Food Insecurity

How Can the Poor Be Helped?

What Is the Future of the US Economy?

Current Controversies Series

Developing Nations

The Elderly

Jobs in America

The Uninsured

"Congress shall make no law . . . abridging the freedom of speech, or of the press."

First Amendment to the US Constitution

The basic foundation of our democracy is the First Amendment guarantee of freedom of expression. The Opposing Viewpoints series is dedicated to the concept of this basic freedom and the idea that it is more important to practice it than to enshrine it.

OPPOSING
VIEWPOINTS®
SERIES

Poverty

Roman Espejo, Book Editor

GREENHAVEN PRESS
A part of Gale, Cengage Learning

GALE
CENGAGE Learning®

Detroit • New York • San Francisco • New Haven, Conn • Waterville, Maine • London

GALE
CENGAGE Learning®

33.36/29.36 6/12

Elizabeth Des Chenes, *Managing Editor*

© 2012 Greenhaven Press, a part of Gale, Cengage Learning.

Gale and Greenhaven Press are registered trademarks used herein under license.

For more information, contact:
Greenhaven Press
27500 Drake Rd.
Farmington Hills, MI 48331-3535
Or you can visit our Internet site at gale.cengage.com

For product information and technology assistance, contact us at

Gale Customer Support, 1-800-877-4253
For permission to use material from this text or product, submit all requests online at www.cengage.com/permissions

Further permissions questions can be emailed to permissionrequest@cengage.com

Articles in Greenhaven Press anthologies are often edited for length to meet page requirements. In addition, original titles of these works are changed to clearly present the main thesis and to explicitly indicate the author's opinion. Every effort is made to ensure that Greenhaven Press accurately reflects the original intent of the authors. Every effort has been made to trace the owners of copyrighted material.

Cover Image copyright © Suzanne Tucker/Shutterstock.com.

LIBRARY OF CONGRESS CATALOGING-IN-PUBLICATION DATA

Poverty / Roman Espejo, book editor.
   p. cm. -- (Opposing viewpoints)
   Includes bibliographical references and index.
   ISBN 978-0-7377-5757-6 (hardcover) -- ISBN 978-0-7377-5758-3 (pbk.)
   1. Poverty--United States. 2. Poverty. I. Espejo, Roman, 1977-
   HC110.P6P5883 2012
   362.50973--dc23

2011048765

Printed in the United States of America
1 2 3 4 5 6 7 16 15 14 13 12

Contents

Chapter 3: How Can Poverty Be Reduced in the United States?

Chapter 4: How Should Global Poverty Be Addressed?

Why Consider Opposing Viewpoints?

> "The only way in which a human being can make some approach to knowing the whole of a subject is by hearing what can be said about it by persons of every variety of opinion and studying all modes in which it can be looked at by every character of mind. No wise man ever acquired his wisdom in any mode but this."
>
> John Stuart Mill

In our media-intensive culture it is not difficult to find differing opinions. Thousands of newspapers and magazines and dozens of radio and television talk shows resound with differing points of view. The difficulty lies in deciding which opinion to agree with and which "experts" seem the most credible. The more inundated we become with differing opinions and claims, the more essential it is to hone critical reading and thinking skills to evaluate these ideas. Opposing Viewpoints books address this problem directly by presenting stimulating debates that can be used to enhance and teach these skills. The varied opinions contained in each book examine many different aspects of a single issue. While examining these conveniently edited opposing views, readers can develop critical thinking skills such as the ability to compare and contrast authors' credibility, facts, argumentation styles, use of persuasive techniques, and other stylistic tools. In short, the Opposing Viewpoints Series is an ideal way to attain the higher-level thinking and reading skills so essential in a culture of diverse and contradictory opinions.

In addition to providing a tool for critical thinking, Opposing Viewpoints books challenge readers to question their own strongly held opinions and assumptions. Most people form their opinions on the basis of upbringing, peer pressure, and personal, cultural, or professional bias. By reading carefully balanced opposing views, readers must directly confront new ideas as well as the opinions of those with whom they disagree. This is not to argue simplistically that everyone who reads opposing views will—or should—change his or her opinion. Instead, the series enhances readers' understanding of their own views by encouraging confrontation with opposing ideas. Careful examination of others' views can lead to the readers' understanding of the logical inconsistencies in their own opinions, perspective on why they hold an opinion, and the consideration of the possibility that their opinion requires further evaluation.

Evaluating Other Opinions

To ensure that this type of examination occurs, Opposing Viewpoints books present all types of opinions. Prominent spokespeople on different sides of each issue as well as well-known professionals from many disciplines challenge the reader. An additional goal of the series is to provide a forum for other, less known, or even unpopular viewpoints. The opinion of an ordinary person who has had to make the decision to cut off life support from a terminally ill relative, for example, may be just as valuable and provide just as much insight as a medical ethicist's professional opinion. The editors have two additional purposes in including these less known views. One, the editors encourage readers to respect others' opinions—even when not enhanced by professional credibility. It is only by reading or listening to and objectively evaluating others' ideas that one can determine whether they are worthy of consideration. Two, the inclusion of such viewpoints encourages the important critical thinking skill of objectively evaluating an author's credentials and bias. This evaluation will illuminate an author's reasons for taking a particular stance on an issue and will aid in readers' evaluation of the author's ideas.

It is our hope that these books will give readers a deeper understanding of the issues debated and an appreciation of the complexity of even seemingly simple issues when good and honest people disagree. This awareness is particularly important in a democratic society such as ours in which people enter into public debate to determine the common good. Those with whom one disagrees should not be regarded as enemies but rather as people whose views deserve careful examination and may shed light on one's own.

Thomas Jefferson once said that "difference of opinion leads to inquiry, and inquiry to truth." Jefferson, a broadly educated man, argued that "if a nation expects to be ignorant and free . . . it expects what never was and never will be." As individuals and as a nation, it is imperative that we consider the opinions of others and examine them with skill and discernment. The Opposing Viewpoints series is intended to help readers achieve this goal.

David L. Bender and Bruno Leone,
Founders

Introduction

"Poverty is not evenly distributed across the American landscape. . . . Poverty is overwhelmingly a rural problem, with the most remote rural places at the greatest disadvantage."

—*Bruce A. Weber,*
professor of agricultural and resource
economics, Oregon State University

As with inner cities, rural areas suffer from high levels of poverty in the United States. "While poverty is not just a rural phenomenon, remote and persistently poor rural counties bear a disproportionate share of our nation's poverty burden,"[1] states the Rural Policy Research Institute (RUPRI). The institute claims that 88 percent of the 386 persistently poor counties are rural and geographically concentrated in the following regions: Appalachia, the Mississippi Delta and southeast, Rio Grande Valley, and Native American reservations in the Great Plains and the Southwest. "Along a continuum of the most urban county to the most rural county, poverty rates are highest in the most remote rural areas," asserts RUPRI.

Appalachia, which stretches from southern New York to northern Mississippi along the Appalachian Mountains, is home to some of the most isolated, poor households in the United States, particularly in the mining communities of Central Appalachia and Kentucky. According to the Appalachian Regional Commission (ARC), the region has a cluster of thirty-one counties with poverty rates ranging from 25.8 to 41.9 percent—at least double the national rate—based on data between 2005 and 2009. Still, the commission points out that the overall level of poverty has improved in Appalachia in the past four decades, from one in three Appalachians in 1965 to

18 percent in 2008. "These gains have transformed the region from one of widespread poverty to one of economic contrasts: Some communities have successfully diversified their economies, while others still require basic infrastructure such as roads and water and sewer systems,"[2] according to the ARC.

With 21.9 percent of the population living below the poverty threshold and ranking last in household income, the state of Mississippi has the highest poverty rate in America. In the Mississippi Delta's Second Congressional District, more than 20 percent of residents receive food stamps. "Even back between 2006 and 2008, while the nation had a 6.8 percent unemployment rate, the Delta held at 12 percent unemployment,"[3] reports Ryan C. Ebersole, a contributor to the grassroots newspaper *People's World*. "The overlap of race, class, and culture has left an impact on the position of the people in the rural south in general and the Delta in particular,"[4] contend John J. Green and Albert B. Nylander III, social science professors at Delta State University. They continue, "While there has been change, especially with the advent of casino gambling and tourist development in the region, contemporary studies show Delta counties with continued high unemployment and poverty rates."

The Rio Grande Valley comprises four counties situated on the southernmost tip of Texas. Eighty-seven percent of the valley's population of one million is of Mexican descent. About 30 percent is estimated to live below the poverty line, with unemployment rates as high as 13.2 percent. Many live in *colonias*, which are low-income neighborhoods and settlements that are unincorporated and may lack adequate infrastructures and basic services. For example, half of rural *colonias* do not have complete plumbing. "Many residents struggle with a lack of available employment or low wages, language and cultural barriers, and resulting health challenges,"[5] states Migrant Health Promotion, which aids rural and farming families.

Poverty is also pervasive on Native American reservations located in the Great Plains and the Southwest. The US Department of Agriculture's Economic Research Service estimates that almost 60 percent of Native Americans outside of metropolitan areas reside in counties that are persistently poor, and only 36 percent of males in poor Native American communities have full-time jobs. "For most tribes, their remotely placed homes and communities frequently stifle viable economic activity,"[6] comments Tom Rodgers, tribal advocate and Blackfoot tribe member.

Some experts propose that the causes of rural poverty are rooted in race and economic inequalities. "The interesting thing that I and others have found is that the same kinds of patterns of control and underinvestment occurred in the Mississippi Delta and along the Mexico-U.S. border,"[7] suggests Cynthia M. Duncan, sociology professor and author of *Worlds Apart: Why Poverty Persists in Rural America*. "The places we see deep, persistent, rural poverty are the places where there is a combination of this economic control and, in many cases, racism," Duncan maintains.

In *Opposing Viewpoints: Poverty*, researchers, advocates, and commentators debate the causes of poverty and more in the following chapters: Is Poverty a Serious Problem in America?, What Causes Poverty in America?, How Can Poverty Be Reduced in the United States?, and How Should Global Poverty Be Addressed? The divergent opinions selected for this volume reflect the polarizing views on poverty today.

Notes

1. Rural Policy Research Institute, "Poverty and Human Services." www.rupri.org.
2. Appalachian Regional Commission, "The Appalachian Region." www.arc.gov.

3. Ryan C. Ebersole, "Third World Mississippi Shows Failure of Conservative Politics," *People's World*, June 24, 2011. http://peoplesworld.org.
4. John J. Green and Albert B. Nylander III, "A Community Based Framework for Understanding Problems and Exploring Alternatives: Connecting Underemployment, Poverty and Access to Health Care in the Mississippi Delta," Rural Poverty Research Center, February 2006. www.rupri.org.
5. Migrant Health Promotion, "The Lower Rio Grande Valley." www.migranthealth.org.
6. Tom Rodgers, "Native American Poverty," Spotlight on Poverty and Opportunity. www.spotlightonpoverty.org.
7. Cynthia M. Duncan, "Why Poverty Persists in Appalachia," *FRONTLINE*, PBS, December 29, 2005. http://www.pbs.org.

OPPOSING VIEWPOINTS® SERIES

CHAPTER 1

Is Poverty a Serious Problem in America?

Chapter Preface

Over the past decade, the rate of domestic child poverty increased 18 percent, and higher levels of poverty hit families with children in thirty-eight states, according to a 2011 study by the Annie E. Casey Foundation, a charity for disadvantaged youths. "The recent recession has wiped out many of the economic gains for children that occurred in the late 1990s,"[1] claims Laura Speer, the foundation's associate director for policy reform and data. "The news about the number of children who were affected by foreclosure in the United States is also very troubling, because these economic challenges greatly hinder the well-being of families and the nation," she maintains. Almost 20 percent of children, or 15 million, are estimated to live in poverty nationwide.

Numerous experts contend that poverty has lasting socioeconomic effects on children. "Persistent poverty among children is of particular concern, as the cumulative effect of being poor may lead to especially negative outcomes and limited opportunities,"[2] contends the Urban Institute, a policy think tank. For example, the institute states that 63 percent of children become adults without experiencing poverty, but 10 percent are perpetually poor, living in poverty at least half of their childhoods. Others argue that poverty traps those who are born into it. "According to one recent estimate, American children born to parents in the bottom fourth of the income distribution have almost a 50 percent chance of staying there—and almost a two-thirds chance of remaining stuck if they're black,"[3] asserts economist Paul Krugman.

Nonetheless, critics dismiss the claim that being poor lasts a lifetime. "When you look at people in the bottom fifth of the economic ladder, only 5 percent are still there 16 years later,"[4] insists Rand Paul, a junior US senator from Kentucky. (Fifths, or quintiles, are used to categorize households by income.) Also, Paul cites US Treasury statistics demonstrating that 86 percent of the bottom fifth jumped to a higher quintile. "The rich are getting richer but the poor are getting richer even faster," he says. In the following chapter, the authors deliberate the scope and severity of poverty in America.

Notes

1. Brad Knickerbocker, "Report: Child Poverty Rate Hits 20 Percent in US as Families Struggle," *Christian Science Monitor*, August 17, 2011. www.csmonitor.com.
2. Caroline Ratcliffe and Signe-Mary McKernan, "Childhood Poverty Persistence: Facts and Consequences," Urban Institute, Brief 14, June 2010. www.urban.org.
3. Paul Krugman, "Poverty Is Poison," *New York Times*, February 18, 2008. www.nytimes.com.
4. Rand Paul, "Poverty Is Not a 'Death Sentence,'" *National Review Online*, September 21, 2011. www.nationalreview.com.

> *"The official poverty rate in 2009 was 14.3 percent—up from 13.2 percent in 2008."*

Census Bureau Measures Show the US Poverty Rate Has Increased

US Census Bureau

Every September, the US Census Bureau reports the number of Americans living in poverty, using data collected in its annual Current Population Survey Annual Social and Economic Supplement (CPS ASEC). In 2009, the weighted average poverty threshold for a family of four was $21,954. In the following viewpoint, the Census Bureau reports that the number of people living in poverty reached 43.6 million that year, the highest number in the five decades in which poverty estimates have been recorded. It states that among ethnic groups, the poverty rate has grown for non-Hispanic whites, Hispanics, and blacks. The Census Bureau also provides poverty statistics on characteristics such as children, regions, residence, work experience, and families.

As you read, consider the following questions:

1. How does the Census Bureau compare the recent economic downturn's effect on poverty rates to previous recessions?

2. How did poverty rates change in the nation's regions, according to the Census Bureau?

3. As stated by the Census Bureau, what do the income-to-poverty ratio and the income deficit or surplus describe?

- The official poverty rate in 2009 was 14.3 percent—up from 13.2 percent in 2008. This was the second statistically significant annual increase in the poverty rate since 2004.

- In 2009, 43.6 million people were in poverty, up from 39.8 million in 2008—the third consecutive annual increase in the number of people in poverty.

- Between 2008 and 2009, the poverty rate increased for non-Hispanic Whites (from 8.6 percent to 9.4 percent), for Blacks (from 24.7 percent to 25.8 percent), and for Hispanics (from 23.2 percent to 25.3 percent). For Asians, the 2009 poverty rate (12.5 percent) was not statistically different from the 2008 poverty rate.

- The poverty rate in 2009 (14.3 percent) was the highest poverty rate since 1994 but was 8.1 percentage points lower than the poverty rate in 1959, the first year for which poverty estimates are available.

- The number of people in poverty in 2009 (43.6 million) is the largest number in the 51 years for which poverty estimates have been published.

- Between 2008 and 2009, the poverty rate increased for children under the age of 18 (from 19.0 percent to 20.7 percent) and people aged 18 to 64 (from 11.7 percent to 12.9 percent), but decreased for people aged 65 and older (from 9.7 percent to 8.9 percent).

Impact of the 2007 Economic Downturn

The poverty rate and the number in poverty increased by 1.9 percentage points and 6.3 million between 2007 and 2009. The increase in the overall poverty rate was:

- Larger than the increase in the poverty rate during the November 1973 to March 1975 recession.

- Smaller than the increase in the poverty rates associated with the January 1980 to July 1980 and July 1981 to November 1982 combined recessions.

Between 2007 and 2009, the child poverty rate and the number in poverty increased by 2.7 percentage points and 2.1 million.

Race and Hispanic Origin

Both the poverty rate and the number in poverty increased for non-Hispanic Whites from 2008 to 2009 (9.4 percent and 18.5 million in 2009—up from 8.6 percent and 17.0 million in 2008). The poverty rate for non-Hispanic Whites was lower than the poverty rates for other race groups. Non-Hispanic Whites accounted for 42.5 percent of the people in poverty, compared with 64.9 percent of the total population.

For Blacks, the poverty rate and the number in poverty increased to 25.8 percent and 9.9 million in 2009, higher than 24.7 percent and 9.4 million in 2008. For Asians, the 2009 poverty rate (12.5 percent) was not statistically different from the 2008 rate, while the number of Asians in poverty increased from 1.6 million in 2008 to 1.7 million in 2009. Both the number in poverty and the poverty rate increased for Hispanics—12.4 million or 25.3 percent were in poverty in 2009, up from 11.0 million or 23.2 percent in 2008.

Age

Between 2008 and 2009, both the poverty rate and the number in poverty increased for people aged 18 to 64 (from 11.7 percent and 22.1 million to 12.9 percent and 24.7 million). Both the poverty rate and the number in poverty decreased for people aged 65 and older (from 9.7 percent and 3.7 million to 8.9 percent and 3.4 million).

Both the poverty rate and the number in poverty increased for children under the age of 18 (from 19.0 percent and 14.1 million in 2008 to 20.7 percent and 15.5 million in 2009). The poverty rate for children was higher than the rates for people aged 18 to 64 and those aged 65 and older. Children comprised 35.5 percent of people in poverty but only 24.5 percent of the total population.

Related children are related to the householder by birth, marriage, or adoption and are not themselves householders or spouses of householders. Both the poverty rate and the number in poverty increased for related children under the age of 18 (from 18.5 percent and 13.5 million in 2008 to 20.1 percent and 14.8 million in 2009). For related children under the age of 18 in families with a female householder, 44.4 percent were in poverty compared with 11.0 percent of related children in married-couple families.

Both the poverty rate and the number in poverty increased for related children under the age of 6 (from 21.3 percent and 5.3 million in 2008 to 23.8 percent and 6.0 million in 2009). Of related children under the age of 6 in families with a female householder, 54.3 percent were in poverty—four times the rate of related children in married-couple families (13.4 percent).

Nativity

Of all people, 87.6 percent were native born and 12.4 percent were foreign born. The poverty rate and the number in poverty for the native-born population increased from 12.6 percent and 33.3 million in 2008 to 13.7 percent and 36.4 million in 2009. Among the foreign-born population, 19.0 percent or 7.2 million people lived in poverty in 2009—up from 17.8 percent or 6.5 million people in 2008.

Of the foreign-born population, 42.6 percent were naturalized U.S. citizens; the remaining were not U.S. citizens. The poverty rate and the number in poverty in 2009 for naturalized U.S. citizens were 10.8 percent and 1.7 million, estimates not statistically different from 2008. The poverty rate and the number in poverty for those who were not U.S. citizens rose to 25.1 percent and 5.4 million in 2009—up from 23.3 percent and 5.0 million in 2008.

Region

The poverty rate increased from 2008 to 2009 in three of the four regions, while all four regions had increases in the number of people in poverty. The Midwest poverty rate increased from 12.4 percent to 13.3 percent, and the number in poverty increased from 8.1 million to 8.8 million; the South increased from 14.3 percent to 15.7 percent and from 15.9 million to 17.6 million; and the West increased from 13.5 percent to 14.8 percent and from 9.6 million to 10.5 million. The 2009 poverty rate for the Northeast was 12.2 percent (not statistically different from the 2008 rate), while the number in poverty increased from 6.3 million in 2008 to 6.7 million in 2009.

Residence

Inside metropolitan statistical areas, the poverty rate and the number of people in poverty were 13.9 percent and 35.7 million in 2009—up from 12.9 percent and 32.6 million in 2008. Among those living outside metropolitan areas, the poverty rate and the number in poverty were 16.6 percent and 7.9 million in 2009—up from 15.1 percent and 7.3 million in 2008.

Between 2008 and 2009, the poverty rate for people in principal cities increased from 17.7 percent to 18.7 percent,

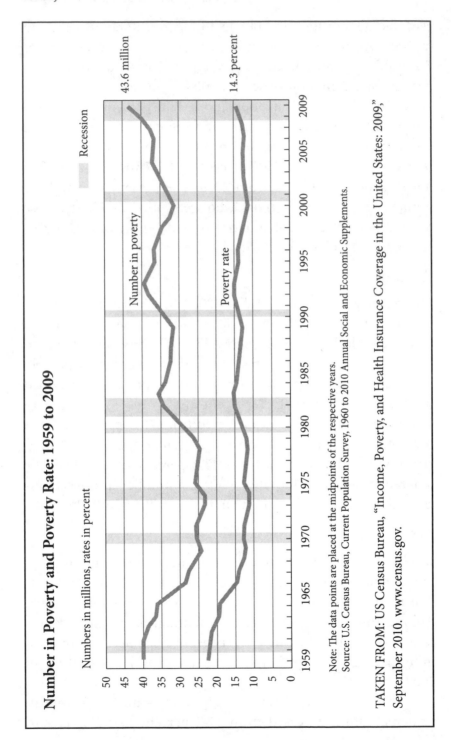

Number in Poverty and Poverty Rate: 1959 to 2009

Numbers in millions, rates in percent

43.6 million

14.3 percent

Number in poverty

Poverty rate

Recession

Note: The data points are placed at the midpoints of the respective years.
Source: U.S. Census Bureau, Current Population Survey, 1960 to 2010 Annual Social and Economic Supplements.

TAKEN FROM: US Census Bureau, "Income, Poverty, and Health Insurance Coverage in the United States: 2009," September 2010. www.census.gov.

while the number in poverty increased from 17.2 million to 18.3 million. Within metropolitan areas, people in poverty were more likely to live in principal cities. While 38.2 percent of all people living in metropolitan areas in 2009 lived in principal cities, 51.2 percent of poor people in metropolitan areas lived in principal cities. For those inside metropolitan areas but not in principal cities, the poverty rate and the number in poverty rose from 9.8 percent and 15.3 million to 11.0 percent and 17.4 million.

Work Experience

Among all workers aged 16 and older, both the poverty rate and the number in poverty increased to 6.9 percent and 10.7 million from 6.4 percent and 10.1 million.

Between 2008 and 2009, the increase in poverty among workers was driven almost entirely by those who worked less than full-time, year-round. Both the percentage and number in poverty increased among less than full-time, year-round workers from 13.5 percent and 7.3 million to 14.5 percent and 8.0 million. For full-time, year-round workers, the percentage and number in poverty in 2009 were not statistically different from 2008—2.7 percent and 2.6 million.

Among those who did not work at least one week last year, the poverty rate and the number in poverty increased to 22.7 percent and 18.9 million in 2009 from 22.0 percent and 17.1 million in 2008.

Families

The poverty rate and the number of families in poverty were 11.1 percent and 8.8 million in 2009 compared with 10.3 percent and 8.1 million in 2008.

The poverty rate and the number of families in poverty increased across all types of families: married-couple families (5.8 percent and 3.4 million in 2009 from 5.5 percent and 3.3 million in 2008); families with a female householder (29.9

percent and 4.4 million in 2009 from 28.7 percent and 4.2 million in 2008); and families with a male householder (16.9 percent and 942,000 in 2009 from 13.8 percent and 723,000 in 2008).

Depth of Poverty

Categorizing a person as "in poverty" or "not in poverty" is one way to describe his or her economic situation. The income-to-poverty ratio and the income deficit or surplus describe additional aspects of economic well-being. While the poverty rate shows the proportion of people with income below the appropriate poverty threshold, the income-to-poverty ratio gauges the depth of poverty. It shows how close a family's income is to their poverty threshold. The income-to-poverty ratio is reported as a percentage that compares a family's or an unrelated person's income with the appropriate poverty threshold. For example, a family with an income-to-poverty ratio of 110 percent has income that is 10 percent above their poverty threshold.

The income deficit or surplus shows how many dollars a family's or an unrelated person's income is below (or above) their poverty threshold. For those with an income deficit, the measure is an estimate of the dollar amount necessary to raise a family's or a person's income to their poverty threshold.

Ratio of Income to Poverty

[The following is] the number and percentage of people with specified income-to-poverty ratios—those below 50 percent of poverty ("Under 0.50"), those below 100 percent of poverty ("Under 1.00," also called "in poverty"), and those below 125 percent of poverty ("Under 1.25").

In 2009, 6.3 percent of all people, or 19.0 million people, had income below one-half of their poverty threshold, up from 5.7 percent and 17.1 million in 2008. This group represented 43.7 percent of the poverty population in 2009. The percentage and number of people with income below 125 percent of their threshold was 18.7 percent and 56.8 million, up from 17.9 percent and 53.8 million in 2008. For children under the age of 18 in 2009, 9.3 percent and 6.9 million lived in families with income below 50 percent of their poverty threshold, up from 8.5 percent and 6.3 million in 2008. The percentage and number of children living in families with income below 125 percent of their poverty threshold in 2009 was 26.3 percent and 19.6 million, up from 25.0 percent and 18.6 million in 2008.

The demographic makeup of the population differs at varying degrees of poverty. Children represented 24.5 percent of the overall population, 35.5 percent of the people in poverty, and 36.3 percent of the people with income below 50 percent of their poverty threshold. On the other hand, the elderly represented 12.7 percent of the overall population, 7.9 percent of the people in poverty, and 5.2 percent of those with income below 50 percent of their poverty threshold. For people with income below 125 percent of their poverty threshold, 34.5 percent were children while 9.7 percent were elderly.

Income Deficit

The income deficit for families in poverty (the difference in dollars between a family's income and its poverty threshold) averaged $9,042 in 2009, which was not statistically different from the 2008 estimate. The average income deficit was larger for families with a female householder ($9,218) than for married-couple families ($8,820).

The average income deficit per capita for families with a female householder ($2,776) was higher than for married-couple families ($2,211). The income deficit per capita is computed by dividing the average deficit by the average number of people in that type of family. Since families with a female householder were smaller, on average, than married-couple families, the larger per capita deficit for female-householder families reflects their smaller average family size as well as their lower average family income.

For unrelated individuals in poverty, the average income deficit was $6,158 in 2009. The $5,926 deficit for women was lower than the $6,443 deficit for men.

> "I have read many reports that simply restate what the government has said without questioning the fact that the metrics it uses to calculate poverty are extremely outdated."

Census Bureau Methods of Measuring Poverty Are Unreliable

David DeGraw

In the following viewpoint, David DeGraw argues that the US Census Bureau uses outdated methods in determining poverty statistics, including the widely reported figure of 43.6 million people in 2009. The Census Bureau's calculations rely on metrics established in 1955, he asserts, failing to take into account the rising costs of living. Moreover, the author contends that the tens of millions of Americans enrolled in unemployment benefits and antipoverty programs and the percentage that lives paycheck to paycheck, which jumped to 77 percent in 2010, are also ignored. DeGraw is an investigative journalist and author of the report The Economic Elite vs. the People of the United States of America.

As you read, consider the following questions:

1. What is the minimum number of people that lived in poverty in 2009, according to DeGraw?

2. What is the author's opinion of the poverty line figure of $22,050 for a family of four?

3. As described in the viewpoint, how has the increase of multifamily households disguised the poverty crisis?

While the shocking new poverty statistics from the Census Bureau indicating that a record 43.6 million Americans lived in poverty in 2009 emphatically demonstrates the severity of the economic crisis, the Census is drastically undercounting this demographic. Apparently the government's poverty statistics are as accurate as its unemployment statistics.

I have read many reports that simply restate what the government has said without questioning the fact that the metrics it uses to calculate poverty are extremely outdated.

News reports say that in 2009 the poverty rate "skyrocketed" to 43.6 million—up from 39.8 million in 2008, which is the largest year-to-year increase and the highest number since statistics have been recorded—putting the poverty rate for 2009 at 14.3 percent. This is obviously a tragedy and horrific news. However, this is also the result of lazy reporting.

Let's revisit the 2008 Census total stating that 39.8 million Americans lived in poverty. It turns out that the National Academy of Sciences did its own study and found that 47.4 million Americans actually lived in poverty in 2008. The Census missed 7.6 million Americans living in poverty that year.

A Long Outdated Method

How did that happen? The Census Bureau uses a long outdated method to calculate the poverty rate. The Census is measuring poverty based on costs of living metrics established back in 1955—55 years ago! They ignore many key factors, such as the increased costs of medical care, child care, education, transportation, and many other basic costs of living. They also don't factor geographically based costs of living. For example, try finding a place to live in New York that costs the same as a place in Florida.

So the Census poverty rate increase of 3.8 million people will put the 2009 National Academy of Sciences (NAS) number at a minimum of 51.2 million Americans. And if the margin of discrepancy is equivalent to the 7.6 million of 2008, we are looking at an NAS number of at least 52 million people for 2009.

Let's also consider the fact that more than 20 million people were on unemployment benefits last year [2009]. A Center on Budget and Policy Priorities analysis concluded that unemployment insurance temporarily kept 3.3 million people out of poverty. Food stamp assistance kept another 2.3 million people out of poverty. If we were to include all of these people, we'd be looking at almost 60 million Americans living in poverty. Which means the government number doesn't account for over 14.1 million Americans in poverty.

The Numbers Behind the Poverty Line

Now let's look at the poverty line these numbers are based on: $22,050 for a family of four. Let me repeat that: $22,050 for a family of four. That breaks down to $5,513 per person, per year. I don't know about you, but I can't imagine living in the United States on $459 per month. That amount will barely get you a good health insurance policy, never mind food, clothes and a roof over your head. No wonder why a record 50.7 million Americans do not have health insurance. (Beware: 50.7 million Americans without health insurance is a government-based number. If you had health insurance for only one day last year, you are not counted in this total.)

Clearly, the Census is setting the income level for its poverty measurement extremely low. If we were to increase that measure by just a small increment, to $25,000 for a family of four, I estimate that the National Academy of Sciences would come up with a number of nearly 100 million Americans in poverty.

Let's also consider the staggering amount of Americans—52 million, roughly 17 percent of the population—who are currently enrolled in "antipoverty" programs. Over 50 million are on Medicaid, 41 million [are] on food stamps, 10 million [are] on unemployment; 4.4 million receive welfare. Not counted in this "antipoverty" total are 30 million children enrolled in the National School Lunch Program. Another metric: if it wasn't for Social Security—note to deficit hawks—20 million more would be added to the poverty total.

The effect of people moving in with family members instead of living on their own has further masked the severity of the poverty crisis. Foreclosures, unemployment, increased cost of education and health insurance have led the average household to grow in size. As Patrick Martin reports:

> The number of multifamily households increased by 11.6 percent from 2008 to 2010, and the proportion of adults 25–34 living with their parents rose from 12.7 percent in 2008 to 13.4 percent in 2010. The poverty rate for these young adults was 8.5 percent when they were considered part of their parents' household, but would have been 43 percent if they had been living on their own.

This trend is currently increasing. Although it is terribly underreported, foreclosure rates continue to rise. We just experienced the worst month of foreclosures in history; the generation just graduating from college is carrying record levels of student-loan debt, and they are being forced into much lower income levels than anticipated, if they can even find employment.

Assets and Liabilities

Another glaring factor clouding our view of poverty in America is that the Census does not calculate a person's assets and liabilities. Considering the massive debts most Americans are carrying, this would make the poverty rate explode. Stephen Crawford and Shawn Fremstad from Reuters concisely summed up this point:

> As Nobel laureates Joseph Stiglitz and Amartya Sen, along with economist Jean-Paul Fitoussi, write in their new book *Mismeasuring Our Lives: Why GDP Doesn't Add Up*, "Income and consumption are crucial for assessing living standards, but in the end they can only be gauged in conjunction with information on wealth." This point is just as relevant to poverty measurement as it is to other measures of living standards.
>
> To understand why this is the case, consider two families: one had an income that puts them a few thousand dollars below the poverty line, which was $22,050 for a family of four in 2009; the other has an income a few thousand dollars above the line. Looking only at income, the first family is worse off than the second.
>
> Now add what the family owns and owes into the mix. Let's say the first family has substantial net equity in its home and moderate liquid savings for a "rainy day," while the latter has no liquid savings or, as is becoming too common these days, has liabilities that dwarf their assets such as an "underwater" mortgage. Using this more comprehensive method, the latter family, despite a modestly higher income, is actually the poorer one.

Living Paycheck to Paycheck

In my analysis, a key metric to judge the overall economic security and hardship level of a country is the percentage of the population living paycheck to paycheck. Anyone who lives paycheck to paycheck can tell you about the stress and psychological impact it has on you when you know your family is one sickness, injury or downsizing away from economic ruin. The employment company CareerBuilder, in partnership with Harris Interactive, conducts an annual survey to determine the percentage of Americans currently living paycheck to paycheck. In 2007, 43 percent fell into this category. In 2008, the number increased to 49 percent. In 2009, the number skyrocketed up to 61 percent.

In their most recent survey, this number exploded to a mind-shattering 77 percent. Yes, 77 percent of Americans are now living paycheck to paycheck. This means in our nation of 310 million citizens, 239 million Americans are one setback away from economic ruin.

So when I hear the government and media tell me that 43.6 million Americans lived in poverty in 2009, while that is horrifying enough, I get extraordinarily frustrated knowing that even that sad statistic is putting a major positive spin on this economic disaster that is still far from over. While the economic top half of 1 percent now fears a "double-dip," the overwhelming majority of Americans are still in the same downward spiral they've been on.

Corporate Profits Are Soaring

For one last missing piece to this equation, corporate profits are soaring while all this devastation is occurring. Despite this economic crisis, it's not like our country doesn't have the money. A recent study done by Capgemini and Merrill Lynch Wealth Management found that a mere 1 percent of Americans are hoarding *$13 trillion* in "investible wealth." Yep, 1 percent of Americans are hoarding *$13 TRILLION* in "investible wealth," and that doesn't even factor in all the money they have hidden in offshore accounts.

As American philosopher John Dewey once said, "There is no such thing as the liberty or effective power of an individual, group, or class, except in relation to the liberties, the effective powers, of other individuals, groups or classes."

The United States now has the highest inequality of wealth in our nation's history. Tens of millions of Americans are wondering how they are going to pay their bills, while the people who caused this crisis are rolling around in $13 trillion. The robber barons have been displaced as America's most despotic and depraved ruling class.

> "The average person identified as 'poor' by the government has a living standard far higher than the public imagines."

Most "Poor" Americans Enjoy a Comfortable Standard of Living

Robert Rector

Robert Rector is a senior research fellow at the Heritage Foundation. In the following viewpoint, Rector maintains that despite the US Census Bureau's reports that more than thirty million Americans live in poverty each year, the vast majority of the "poor" have high living standards, including cable televisions, cars, modern conveniences, homes in good condition, and good nutrition. Inaccurate accounts of poverty not only exaggerate the levels of hardship, he points out, but also underestimate how much the federal government spends on the poor for welfare aid and social services.

As you read, consider the following questions:

1. What percentage of poor households own their own homes, as stated by the author?

2. What would occur if government spending on the poor were converted to cash, as stated by Rector?

3. How much does the typical poor family with children work, as claimed by Rector?

Today [September 10, 2009], the U.S. Census Bureau will release its annual poverty report. The report is expected to show an increase in poverty in 2008 due to the onset of the recession. It is no surprise that poverty goes up in a recession. What is surprising is that every year for nearly three decades, in good economic times and bad, Census has reported more than 30 million Americans living in poverty.

What does it mean to be "poor" in America? For the average reader, the word poverty implies significant physical hardship—for example, the lack of a warm, adequate home, nutritious food, or reasonable clothing for one's children. By that measure, very few of the 30 million plus individuals defined as "living in poverty" by the government are actually poor. Real hardship does occur, but it is limited in scope and severity.

The average person identified as "poor" by the government has a living standard far higher than the public imagines. According to the government's own surveys, the typical "poor" American has cable or satellite TV, two color TVs, and a DVD player or VCR. He has air-conditioning, a car, a microwave, a refrigerator, a stove, and a clothes washer and dryer. He is able to obtain medical care when needed. His home is in good repair and is not overcrowded. By his own report, his family is not hungry, and he had sufficient funds in the past year to meet his family's essential needs. While this individual's life is not affluent, it is far from the images of dire poverty conveyed by liberal activists and politicians.

Defined as "Poor"

Various government reports contain the following facts about persons defined as "poor" by the Census Bureau:

- Nearly 40 percent of all poor households actually own their own homes. On average, this is a three-bedroom house with one-and-a-half baths, a garage, and a porch or patio.

- Eighty-four percent of poor households have air-conditioning. By contrast, in 1970, only 36 percent of the entire U.S. population enjoyed air-conditioning.

- Nearly two-thirds of the poor have cable or satellite TV.

- Only 6 percent of poor households are overcrowded; two-thirds have more than two rooms per person.

- The typical poor American has as much or more living space than the average individual living in most European countries. (These comparisons are to the average citizens in foreign countries, not to those classified as poor.)

- Nearly three-quarters of poor households own a car; 31 percent own two or more cars.

- Ninety-eight percent of poor households have a color television; two-thirds own two or more color televisions.

- Eighty-two percent own microwave ovens; 67 percent have a DVD player; 73 percent have a VCR; 47 percent have a computer.

- The average intake of protein, vitamins, and minerals by poor children is indistinguishable from that of children in the upper middle class. Poor boys today at ages 18 and 19 are actually taller and heavier than middle-class boys of similar age were in the late 1950s. They are a full inch taller and ten pounds heavier than the GIs [U.S. service members] who stormed the beaches of Normandy during World War II.

Conventional accounts of poverty not only exaggerate hardship, they also underestimate government spending on the poor. In 2008, federal and state governments spent $714 billion (or 5 percent of the total economy) on means-tested welfare aid, providing cash, food, housing, medical care, and targeted social services to poor and low-income Americans. (This sum does not include Social Security or Medicare.) If converted into cash, this aid would be nearly four times the amount needed to eliminate poverty in the U.S. by raising the incomes of all poor households above the federal poverty levels.

Ignoring the Welfare State

How can the government spend so much and still have such high levels of apparent poverty? The answer is that, in measuring poverty and inequality, Census ignores almost the entire welfare state. Census deems a household poor if its income falls below federally specified levels. But in its regular measurements, Census counts only around 4 percent of total welfare spending as "income." Because of this, government spending on the poor can expand almost infinitely without having any detectable impact on official poverty or inequality.

Also missing in most Washington discussions about the poor is an acknowledgement of the behavioral causes of official poverty. For example, families with children become poor primarily because of low levels of parental work and high levels of out-of-wedlock childbearing with accompanying single parenthood.

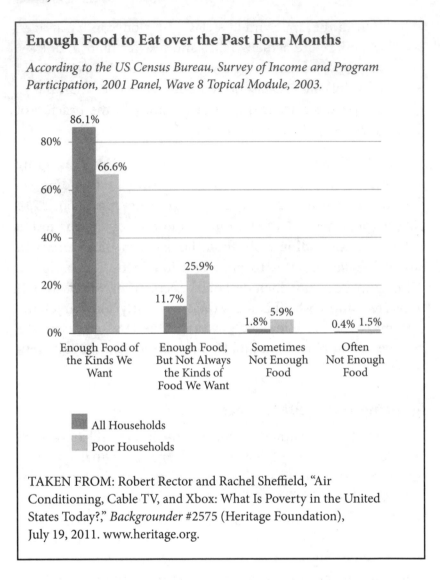

Enough Food to Eat over the Past Four Months

According to the US Census Bureau, Survey of Income and Program Participation, 2001 Panel, Wave 8 Topical Module, 2003.

- All Households
- Poor Households

TAKEN FROM: Robert Rector and Rachel Sheffield, "Air Conditioning, Cable TV, and Xbox: What Is Poverty in the United States Today?," *Backgrounder* #2575 (Heritage Foundation), July 19, 2011. www.heritage.org.

Even in the best economic times, the typical poor family with children has, on average, only 16 hours of work per week. Little work equals little income equals more poverty. Nearly two-thirds of poor children live in single-parent homes, a condition that has been promoted by the astonishing growth of out-of-wedlock childbearing in low-income communities.

When the War on Poverty began, 7 percent of American children were born outside marriage; today the number is 39 percent.

President [Barack] Obama is pursuing his agenda to "spread the wealth" through massive hikes in welfare spending financed by unprecedented increases in the federal debt. Before we further expand the welfare state and pile even greater indebtedness on our children, we need a more honest assessment of current antipoverty spending and the actual living conditions of the "poor."

> *"Despite working hard, too many American families are struggling to get by, advance to the middle class and provide a secure future for their children."*

The Working Poor Are Not Getting By in America

Working Poor Families Project

In the following viewpoint, the Working Poor Families Project asserts that many low-income working families struggle and do not earn enough for financial security. Working for poverty-level wages and inadequate benefits, adults in these households, the project claims, pay much greater portions of their salaries to rent, are much less likely to have health insurance, and do not have the skills and education to succeed in the current economy. Therefore, the project recommends that federal policies advance the skills of working adults and help low-income families meet their basic needs. The Working Poor Families Project is a national initiative that advocates for low-income working families.

As you read, consider the following questions:

1. How does the project address the myth that low-income working families do not work?

2. What national figures does the project cite for working adults and their education and skills?

3. What were the numbers of low-income working families in the United States in 2006, as stated by the project?

America's low-income working families typically include men and women who work as cashiers, custodians, child care workers, health care aides and security guards—workers who constitute the backbone of an increasingly service-based economy. They work hard, pay taxes and strive to achieve a brighter economic future for their families. But they lack the earnings necessary to meet their basic needs—a struggle exacerbated by soaring prices for food, gas, health care and education.

One out of four working families with children—a total of 9.6 million working families—is low-income.... These families pay a higher percentage of their income for housing than other working families, are far less likely to have health insurance, and often lack the education and skills that enable others to succeed in today's skills-driven economy.

At the same time, low-income working families, contrary to popular myth, work hard. Adults in low-income working families worked on average 2,552 hours per year in 2006, the equivalent of almost one and a quarter full-time workers. Despite working hard, too many American families are struggling to get by, advance to the middle class and provide a secure future for their children.

Since the Working Poor Families Project's last report in 2004, the conditions for working families in America have worsened.... The number of low-income working families with children has increased by more than 350,000. This increase is alarming as it occurred at a time of solid national economic growth.

Income inequality increased among working families by almost 10 percent in recent years as indicated by the widening

Hard Work Cures Poverty?

While the United States has enjoyed unprecedented affluence, low-wage employees have been testing the American doctrine that hard work cures poverty. Some have found that work works. Others have learned that it doesn't. Moving in and out of jobs that demand much and pay little, many people tread just above the official poverty line, dangerously close to the edge of destitution. An inconvenience to an affluent family—minor car trouble, a brief illness, disrupted child care—is a crisis to them, for it can threaten their ability to stay employed. They spend everything and save nothing. They are always behind on their bills. They have minuscule bank accounts or none at all, and so pay more fees and higher interest rates than more secure Americans. Even when the economy is robust, many wander through a borderland of struggle, never getting very far from where they started. When the economy weakens, they slip back toward the precipice.

David K. Shipler,
The Working Poor: Invisible in America.
New York: Vintage Books, 2005.

gap between the share of income received by the highest-earning working families and the share received by the least affluent ones. This growing disparity between poor and wealthy families affects more and more children, with more than 21 million children living in a low-income working family. And more low-income working families find it difficult to secure affordable housing or access to health care.

One key factor is that America's educational systems continue to poorly prepare workers for jobs requiring higher skills. At the same time, the economy is comprised of a larger share of low-paying jobs, with an increase of 4.7 million jobs paying a poverty-level wage from 2002 to 2006.

A major challenge moving ahead will be to raise the education and skills of America's workers to meet the needs of the changing economy. Almost one-half of all job openings require more than a high school education, yet as noted in the report of the National Commission on Adult Literacy [*Reach Higher, America: Overcoming Crisis in the U.S. Workforce*], 88 million adult workers are not prepared for these positions; 25 million of these adult workers lack a high school degree or its equivalent. At the same time, combined federal and state government resources for such programs as adult education or skills development serve approximately one-tenth of the need.

Experience shows that public policies that promote education and skills development, quality jobs, health care and family leave are effective ways to foster family economic security. With elections preparing to reshape administrations in Washington and many state capitals, fresh and immediate attention to these issues is needed.

A Fifty-State Economic Issue

A new administration in Washington will have the opportunity to strengthen federal policies on behalf of America's working families. But state resources and policies remain critical to the economic prospects of working families. And states have many reasons to devote attention to these families' needs.

The problem is sizeable.

As measured in 2006, all states have a significant number of low-income working families. California and Texas each have more than a million low-income working families, while Florida and New York each have more than 500,000. Even the five states with the smallest percentage of such families (New

Hampshire, Maryland, Connecticut, Massachusetts and New Jersey) are home to roughly 500,000 of these families collectively.

In 13 states, 33 percent or more of working families are low income, and two states, Mississippi and New Mexico, have 40 percent or more. In eight states, 40 percent or more of the children of working adults reside in low-income families.

Economic opportunity is not equally shared.

In 13 states, 50 percent or more of minority working families are low income. By comparison, there is not one state where white working families represent half of the low-income population. At most, in West Virginia, one-third of white working families are low income.

In seven states, more than one-third of low-income working families have a parent without a high school degree, with one state, California, exceeding 50 percent. Among working families that are not low income, only 10 percent nationally have a parent who did not complete high school.

Too many jobs offer low wages and inadequate benefits.

Nationally, more than one in five jobs, or 22 percent, is in an occupation paying wages that fall below the federal poverty threshold. In eight states, more than one-third of all jobs are in poverty-wage occupations.

Nationally, 39 percent of low-income working families include a parent without health insurance. Fifteen states have 40 percent or more; two states, Texas and New Mexico, have 50 percent or more.

Conditions in the states vary substantially across the country as do state commitments to working families. State policies related to the minimum wage, taxes, financial aid for postsecondary education, health care and paid family leave affect the ability of working families to prosper and achieve economic advancement. All states can strengthen their policies to better serve low-income working families.

A Call for Stronger Policies

Federal policy has not adequately addressed the array of issues critical to low-income working families, and too few states have focused on the needs of working families or quality of jobs. However, some states have taken actions that provide direction for other states to follow.

States are developing innovative policies.

State governments are strengthening policies that affect low-income working families in two key ways: 1) investing in programs to advance the skills of adult workers; and 2) helping to meet the basic household needs of working families.

States are investing in adult workers primarily by improving education and skill-development policies that help workers compete in the new economy. This includes working with employers to raise the basic education and literacy levels of workers and allocating financial aid to adults seeking to attend community colleges. Nationwide efforts, including the National Governors Association's Pathways to Advancement, Charles Stewart Mott Foundation's State Sector Strategies, Ford Foundation's Bridges to Opportunity and the Joyce Foundation's Shifting Gears initiatives, have supported comprehensive policy reform at the highest levels of state government.

To meet the needs of working families, states are strengthening policies related to pay and benefits. Half of the states now maintain a minimum wage above the federal wage standard, and some states are doing more to provide paid parental leave for family and medical needs and to lower tax rates on the working poor. A number of states have recently created commissions to identify better policies to reduce family poverty.

> *"The top 1 percent have the best houses, the best educations, the best doctors, and the best lifestyles, but there is one thing that money doesn't seem to have bought: an understanding that their fate is bound up with how the other 99 percent live."*

The Gap Between the Rich and Poor Is Widening

Joseph E. Stiglitz

Joseph E. Stiglitz is University Professor at Columbia University, a Nobel laureate in economics, and author of Freefall: America, Free Markets, and the Sinking of the World Economy. *In the following viewpoint, he contends that the top 1 percent now earn almost a quarter of income and control 40 percent of wealth in the United States, while wages have declined for the middle class. According to Stiglitz, this growing income gap represents diminished opportunities for Americans; the undermining of the economy's efficiency through monopolies and preferential tax treatment; and lower investments in public infrastructure, re-*

search, and education. Ultimately, the author warns that extreme economic inequality will result in social and political upheaval.

As you read, consider the following questions:

1. According to Stiglitz, how much did incomes rise for the top 1 percent and fall for the middle class?

2. In what ways has the top 1 percent created so much income inequality, in Stiglitz's view?

3. What is important about "self-interest properly understood," as told by the author?

It's no use pretending that what has obviously happened has not in fact happened. The upper 1 percent of Americans are now taking in nearly a quarter of the nation's income every year. In terms of wealth rather than income, the top 1 percent control 40 percent. Their lot in life has improved considerably. Twenty-five years ago, the corresponding figures were 12 percent and 33 percent. One response might be to celebrate the ingenuity and drive that brought good fortune to these people, and to contend that a rising tide lifts all boats. That response would be misguided. While the top 1 percent have seen their incomes rise 18 percent over the past decade, those in the middle have actually seen their incomes fall. For men with only high school degrees, the decline has been precipitous—12 percent in the last quarter century alone. All the growth in recent decades—and more—has gone to those at the top. In terms of income equality, America lags behind any country in the old, ossified Europe that President George W. Bush used to deride. Among our closest counterparts are Russia with its oligarchs and Iran. While many of the old centers of inequality in Latin America, such as Brazil, have been striving in recent years, rather successfully, to improve the plight of the poor and reduce gaps in income, America has allowed inequality to grow.

Economists long ago tried to justify the vast inequalities that seemed so troubling in the mid-19th century—inequalities that are but a pale shadow of what we are seeing in America today. The justification they came up with was called "marginal-productivity theory." In a nutshell, this theory associated higher incomes with higher productivity and a greater contribution to society. It is a theory that has always been cherished by the rich. Evidence for its validity, however, remains thin. The corporate executives who helped bring on the recession of the past three years—whose contribution to our society, and to their own companies, has been massively negative—went on to receive large bonuses. In some cases, companies were so embarrassed about calling such rewards "performance bonuses" that they felt compelled to change the name to "retention bonuses" (even if the only thing being retained was bad performance). Those who have contributed great positive innovations to our society, from the pioneers of genetic understanding to the pioneers of the Information Age, have received a pittance compared with those responsible for the financial innovations that brought our global economy to the brink of ruin.

Not the Size of the Pie

Some people look at income inequality and shrug their shoulders. So what if this person gains and that person loses? What matters, they argue, is not how the pie is divided but the size of the pie. That argument is fundamentally wrong. An economy in which *most* citizens are doing worse year after year—an economy like America's—is not likely to do well over the long haul. There are several reasons for this.

First, growing inequality is the flip side of something else: shrinking opportunity. Whenever we diminish equality of opportunity, it means that we are not using some of our most valuable assets—our people—in the most productive way possible. Second, many of the distortions that lead to inequality—such as those associated with monopoly power and preferential tax treatment for special interests—undermine the efficiency of the economy. This new inequality goes on to create new distortions, undermining efficiency even further. To give just one example, far too many of our most talented young people, seeing the astronomical rewards, have gone into finance rather than into fields that would lead to a more productive and healthy economy.

Third, and perhaps most important, a modern economy requires "collective action"—it needs government to invest in infrastructure, education, and technology. The United States and the world have benefited greatly from government-sponsored research that led to the Internet, to advances in public health, and so on. But America has long suffered from an underinvestment in infrastructure (look at the condition of our highways and bridges, our railroads and airports), in basic research, and in education at all levels. Further cutbacks in these areas lie ahead.

None of this should come as a surprise—it is simply what happens when a society's wealth distribution becomes lopsided. The more divided a society becomes in terms of wealth, the more reluctant the wealthy become to spend money on common needs. The rich don't need to rely on government for parks or education or medical care or personal security—they can buy all these things for themselves. In the process, they become more distant from ordinary people, losing whatever empathy they may once have had. They also worry about strong government—one that could use its powers to adjust the balance, take some of their wealth, and invest it for the common good. The top 1 percent may complain about the kind of government we have in America, but in truth they like it just fine: too gridlocked to redistribute, too divided to do anything but lower taxes.

The Top 1 Percent Want Inequality

Economists are not sure how to fully explain the growing inequality in America. The ordinary dynamics of supply and demand have certainly played a role: laborsaving technologies have reduced the demand for many "good" middle-class, blue-collar jobs. Globalization has created a worldwide market-place, pitting expensive unskilled workers in America against cheap unskilled workers overseas. Social changes have also played a role—for instance, the decline of unions, which once represented a third of American workers and now represent about 12 percent.

But one big part of the reason we have so much inequality is that the top 1 percent want it that way. The most obvious example involves tax policy. Lowering tax rates on capital gains, which is how the rich receive a large portion of their income, has given the wealthiest Americans close to a free ride. Monopolies and near monopolies have always been a source of economic power—from [industrialist] John D. Rockefeller at the beginning of the last century to [Microsoft chairman] Bill Gates at the end. Lax enforcement of antitrust laws, especially during Republican administrations, has been a godsend to the top 1 percent. Much of today's inequality is due to manipulation of the financial system, enabled by changes in the rules that have been bought and paid for by the financial industry itself—one of its best investments ever. The government lent money to financial institutions at close to 0 percent interest and provided generous bailouts on favorable terms when all else failed. Regulators turned a blind eye to a lack of transparency and to conflicts of interest.

When you look at the sheer volume of wealth controlled by the top 1 percent in this country, it's tempting to see our growing inequality as a quintessentially American achievement—we started way behind the pack, but now we're doing inequality on a world-class level. And it looks as if we'll be building on this achievement for years to come, because what made it possible is self-reinforcing. Wealth begets power, which begets more wealth. During the savings-and-loan scandal of the 1980s—a scandal whose dimensions, by today's standards, seem almost quaint—the banker Charles Keating was asked by a congressional committee whether the $1.5 million he had spread among a few key elected officials could actually buy influence. "I certainly hope so," he replied. The Supreme Court, in its recent *Citizens United [v. Federal Election Commission]* case, has enshrined the right of corporations to buy government, by removing limitations on campaign spending. The personal and the political are today in perfect alignment. Virtually all U.S. senators, and most of the representatives in the House, are members of the top 1 percent when they arrive, are kept in office by money from the top 1 percent, and know that if they serve the top 1 percent well they will be rewarded by the top 1 percent when they leave office. By and large, the key executive branch policy makers on trade and economic policy also come from the top 1 percent. When pharmaceutical companies receive a trillion-dollar gift—through legislation prohibiting the government, the largest buyer of drugs, from bargaining over price—it should not come as cause for wonder. It should not make jaws drop that a tax bill cannot emerge from Congress unless big tax cuts are put in place for the wealthy. Given the power of the top 1 percent, this is the way you would *expect* the system to work.

Distorting Society

America's inequality distorts our society in every conceivable way. There is, for one thing, a well-documented lifestyle effect—people outside the top 1 percent increasingly live beyond their means. Trickle-down economics may be a chimera, but trickle-down behaviorism is very real. Inequality massively distorts our foreign policy. The top 1 percent rarely serve in the military—the reality is that the "all-volunteer" army does not pay enough to attract their sons and daughters, and patriotism goes only so far. Plus, the wealthiest class feels no pinch from higher taxes when the nation goes to war: Borrowed money will pay for all that. Foreign policy, by definition, is about the balancing of national interests and national resources. With the top 1 percent in charge, and paying no price, the notion of balance and restraint goes out the window. There is no limit to the adventures we can undertake; corporations and contractors stand only to gain. The rules of economic globalization are likewise designed to benefit the rich: They encourage competition among countries for *business*, which drives down taxes on corporations, weakens health and environmental protections, and undermines what used to be viewed as the "core" labor rights, which include the right to collective bargaining. Imagine what the world might look like if the rules were designed instead to encourage competition among countries for *workers*. Governments would compete in providing economic security, low taxes on ordinary wage earners, good education, and a clean environment—things workers care about. But the top 1 percent don't need to care.

Or, more accurately, they think they don't. Of all the costs imposed on our society by the top 1 percent, perhaps the greatest is this: the erosion of our sense of identity, in which fair play, equality of opportunity, and a sense of community are so important. America has long prided itself on being a fair society, where everyone has an equal chance of getting ahead, but the statistics suggest otherwise: The chances of a poor citizen, or even a middle-class citizen, making it to the top in America are smaller than in many countries of Europe. The cards are stacked against them. It is this sense of an unjust system without opportunity that has given rise to the conflagrations in the Middle East: Rising food prices and growing and persistent youth unemployment simply served as kindling. With youth unemployment in America at around 20 percent (and in some locations, and among some sociodemographic groups, at twice that); with one out of six Americans desiring a full-time job not able to get one; with one out of seven Americans on food stamps (and about the same number suffering from "food insecurity")—given all this, there is ample evidence that something has blocked the vaunted "trickling down" from the top 1 percent to everyone else. All of this is having the predictable effect of creating alienation—voter turnout among those in their 20s in the last election stood at 21 percent, comparable to the unemployment rate.

Bound Up with the 99 Percent

In recent weeks we have watched people taking to the streets by the millions to protest political, economic, and social conditions in the oppressive societies they inhabit. Governments have been toppled in Egypt and Tunisia. Protests have erupted in Libya, Yemen, and Bahrain. The ruling families elsewhere in the region look on nervously from their air-conditioned penthouses—will they be next? They are right to worry. These are societies where a minuscule fraction of the population—less than 1 percent—controls the lion's share of the wealth; where wealth is a main determinant of power; where entrenched corruption of one sort or another is a way of life; and where the wealthiest often stand actively in the way of policies that would improve life for people in general.

As we gaze out at the popular fervor in the streets, one question to ask ourselves is this: When will it come to America? In important ways, our own country has become like one of these distant, troubled places.

[French political thinker] Alexis de Tocqueville once described what he saw as a chief part of the peculiar genius of American society—something he called "self-interest properly understood." The last two words were the key. Everyone possesses self-interest in a narrow sense: I want what's good for me right now! Self-interest "properly understood" is different. It means appreciating that paying attention to everyone else's self-interest—in other words, the common welfare—is in fact a precondition for one's own ultimate well-being. Tocqueville was not suggesting that there was anything noble or idealistic about this outlook—in fact, he was suggesting the opposite. It was a mark of American pragmatism. Those canny Americans understood a basic fact: Looking out for the other guy isn't just good for the soul—it's good for business.

The top 1 percent have the best houses, the best educations, the best doctors, and the best lifestyles, but there is one thing that money doesn't seem to have bought: an understanding that their fate is bound up with how the other 99 percent live. Throughout history, this is something that the top 1 percent eventually do learn. Too late.

> *"There is little evidence of a significant or sustained increase in the inequality of U.S. incomes, wages, consumption, or wealth over the last 20 years."*

The Gap Between the Rich and Poor Is Not Widening

Terence Corcoran

In the following viewpoint, Terence Corcoran opposes the argument that the income divide is growing between the rich and the middle and lower classes. Corcoran alleges that the figures used to support a great inequality of wealth measure pretax income and do not count benefits such as Social Security, welfare, and unemployment, resulting in underreported lower-class incomes. He further claims that the pretax income increases of the top 10 percent of income earners can be attributed to the top 1 percent; incomes in the remaining 9 percent have remained flat. Corcoran is editor and columnist for the Financial Post *section of the Canadian newspaper* National Post.

As you read, consider the following questions:

1. In what context are pretax incomes meaningless, in Corcoran's opinion?

2. What is the finding after incomes of taxpayers are adjusted for regional costs of living differences, as told by the author?

3. What has the Organisation for Economic Co-operation and Development (OECD) stated about the American tax system?

For several years now the American Left has been fixated on the idea that the United States has become a divided nation in which an aristocracy of the rich, the super rich and the stinking rich have subjugated the poor, the middle class and everybody else, turning America into the equivalent of some pre-Robespierreian France. This Marxist class war message was embedded in President Barack Obama's first budget: "For the better part of three decades, a disproportionate share of the nation's wealth has been accumulated by the very wealthy."

The basis for that claim and others in the Obama budget is the work of Thomas Piketty and Emmanuel Saez, two economists who in recent years have become the darlings of activists and politicians whose prime aim appears to be to foment class envy and promote new higher tax rates and bigger government. One of their graphs appeared in the Obama budget, apparently showing that the "top 1% of earners have been increasing their share of national income" to the point where the stinking rich 1% earn 20% of the total, double their share from 10% in 1980.

Other Piketty-Saez graphs, variation on the same theme, often make their way into the media, including the *National Post*. On the editorial pages of the *Post* last Wednesday [in September 2010], one of their iconic illustrations was used to support an op-ed by journalist Timothy Noah and his theme that America had become the United States of Inequality. The graph . . . appears to prove that income disparity is growing in the United States, with the top 10% of income earners taking up almost 50% of national income, up from 35% in 1980.

Mr. Noah's op-ed was first published by *Slate* as part of a series in which Mr. Noah weaves a tangled Wikipedian web of quotations, citations and statistics around the graph to prove that the level of inequality and disparity today in the United States is historical. It takes the country back to the early 20th century, a time when "the socialist movement was at its historic peak, a wave of anarchist bombings was terrorizing the nation's industrialists." In American history, says Mr. Noah, "there has never been a time when class warfare seemed more imminent."

The obvious implication of Mr. Noah's op-ed is that the U.S. has reverted back to some barbarian time—if only the people knew it. "Growing income inequality is deeply worrying," said Mr. Noah. It "may represent the most significant change in American society in your lifetime—and it's not a change for the better."

Unfortunately for Mr. Noah, as he laments frequently, the American public doesn't quite buy the Piketty-Saez inequality scare. Nor do many economists outside of the [economist] Paul Krugman circle Mr. Noah seems to be traveling in. The Tea Party movement seems to be more concerned about taxes on the middle class than the rise of inequality.

Distorting the Picture

The graph itself reeks of implausibility—the huge dip during the Second World War, the flat line through the 1940s to 1970s, and the sudden escalation over the last 30 years. For one thing, it measures pretax market income, excludes government transfers, and includes capital gains.

Pretax income levels are essentially meaningless in an economy where massive tax redistributions alter the final outcome. Excluding government transfers—Social Security, welfare, Medicare, unemployment and other benefits—means

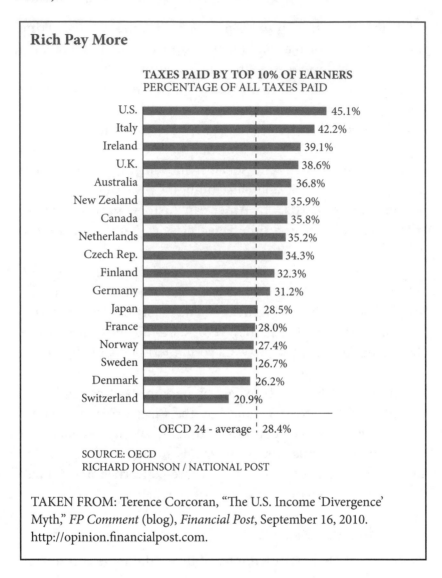

Rich Pay More

TAXES PAID BY TOP 10% OF EARNERS
PERCENTAGE OF ALL TAXES PAID

Country	Percentage
U.S.	45.1%
Italy	42.2%
Ireland	39.1%
U.K.	38.6%
Australia	36.8%
New Zealand	35.9%
Canada	35.8%
Netherlands	35.2%
Czech Rep.	34.3%
Finland	32.3%
Germany	31.2%
Japan	28.5%
France	28.0%
Norway	27.4%
Sweden	26.7%
Denmark	26.2%
Switzerland	20.9%

OECD 24 - average : 28.4%

SOURCE: OECD
RICHARD JOHNSON / NATIONAL POST

TAKEN FROM: Terence Corcoran, "The U.S. Income 'Divergence' Myth," *FP Comment* (blog), *Financial Post*, September 16, 2010. http://opinion.financialpost.com.

that lower income levels are grossly understated, especially since such transfers surged through the welfare-state expansions of the middle of the 20th century.

The inclusion of capital gains and other business income also creates a distortion. It is also impossible to compare income levels over a century when massive changes in tax regimes radically shifted income reporting and strategies.

How badly does this Piketty-Saez graph distort the picture? How far are these numbers from the reality of income distribution across the United States? And, as a result, how far away is America from Mr. Noah's implied return to a new state of class warfare and, perhaps, the rise of some modern-day Marxist extremist movement?

The economic literature is full of debate, most of it in rejection of the basic premise that inequality has been dramatically on the rise. Prof. Robert J. Gordon of Northwestern University, in a 2009 paper ("Has the Rise in American Inequality Been Exaggerated?") found contrary evidence throughout the literature. He also conducted his own review of income inequality arguments to support his conclusion that the inequality gap is grossly exaggerated. Making adjustments to more conventional measures—median household income versus productivity—Prof. Gordon found that "over the three decades [from 1979 to 2007] the alternative gap measure grew at an annual rate barely one-10th as fast as the conventional gap measure."

When incomes of taxpayers are adjusted for regional cost of living differences, the finding is that inequality—such as it was—stopped growing more than 15 years ago.

The Piketty-Saez graph also contains another distortion. All of the increase in pretax income of the top 10% share can be attributed to the top 1% of income earners. Thanks in part to tax rules and to a burgeoning economy that pushed financial, entertainment and sports industry salaries to new highs, only the top portion of the income ladder recorded huge gains in pretax income. The tax-induced and regulation-promoted use of stock options also boosted the incomes of the top 1%. But the incomes of the group immediately below the top 1%—the other nine percentage points of top income earners—did not increase their share of incomes over the same period. Between 1927 and 2006, Prof. Gordon shows their share to be flat—despite tax law changes that encouraged stock options.

But again, these are pretax calculations. Alan Reynolds, of the Cato Institute, says the whole Piketty-Saez methodology is flawed and useless. Based on his calculations, using disposable after-tax income as a basis and including transfers from government, there has been no change in U.S. income inequality over the last decades.

Based on disposable income (after tax, after transfers), Mr. Reynolds says there has been no increase in inequality since 1987. "Aside from stock market windfalls . . . there is little evidence of a significant or sustained increase in the inequality of U.S. incomes, wages, consumption or wealth over the last 20 years." With the stock market crash of 2008 and reversals in other markets, any recent blips in inequality measures will have been wiped out by now.

As for the period prior to 1980, Mr. Reynolds says no real comparisons can be made since major changes in tax laws in 1986 and 1993 created radical changes in incentives that promoted stock options and income-shifting behaviour.

Punish the Rich and Reward the Poor

Even though the Piketty-Saez version of income inequality history may be shaky, it is being used explicitly to promote higher taxes on the rich. The two economists, in a paper last October [2009], said the inequality indicators suggest there is great new "tax capacity" among the rich. Increased taxes on the top income group "would yield appreciable revenue that could be deployed to fund public goods and redistribution."

Tax the rich, keep taxes high, don't cut taxes: that's the underlying message from the whole exercise—from Mr. Noah to Professors Piketty and Saez to Barack Obama. The United States is slipping into a state of gross income inequality, worse than most other countries. Time for a regime change that will punish the rich and reward the poor.

Meanwhile, the OECD [Organisation for Economic Cooperation and Development] has described the U.S. tax system as one of the most equitable. The United States, it said in a 2008 report, "has the most progressive tax system and collects the largest share of taxes from the richest 10% of the population." Even if America has more rich than other nations, it does more to redistribute than others. There's more to redistribute.

Which leads us to other subjects. Why, for example, does inequality of incomes—before or after tax—even matter in a market economy where no kings rule by force and no aristocracy plunders the people?

Periodical and Internet Sources Bibliography

The following articles have been selected to supplement the diverse views presented in this chapter.

Kat Aaron and Lynne Perri	"Working, but Still Poor," *New America Media*, September 14, 2011. http://newamericamedia .org.
Gary S. Becker and Kevin M. Murphy	"The Upside of Income Equality," *American*, May/June 2007. www.american.com.
Dave Gilson and Carolyn Perot	"It's the Inequality, Stupid," *Mother Jones*, March/April 2011. http://motherjones.com.
Ken Herman	"American Hardship Comes with Modern Conveniences," *Austin-American Statesman*, October 5, 2010. www.statesman.com.
Tami Luhby	"Faces of Poverty," *CNN Money*, September 20, 2011. http://money.cnn.com.
Ileana Johnson Paugh	"Being Poor in America," *Canada Free Press*, August 1, 2011. www.canadafreepress.com.
Yves Smith	"Income Inequality Is Bad for Rich People Too," *Salon*, August 11, 2011. www.salon.com.
Sabrina Tavernise	"Soaring Poverty Casts Spotlight on 'Lost Decade,'" *New York Times*, September 13, 2011. www.nytimes.com.
Will Wilkinson	"Thinking Clearly About Economic Inequality," *Policy Analysis*, no. 640, July 14, 2009. www .cato.org.
Tim Worstall	"The New US Poverty Numbers: Everyone, Just Everyone, Gets This Wrong," *Forbes*, September 13, 2011. www.forbes.com.

CHAPTER 2

What Causes Poverty in America?

Chapter Preface

As a cause of poverty, lack of education is frequently cited by policy makers and researchers alike. "People in poverty tend to stay poor and have low levels of formal education generation after generation,"[1] observes poverty expert Donna M. Beegle, who founded the nonprofit organization Poverty-Bridge and grew up impoverished in a migrant family. "With poverty and illiteracy continuing to be passed down this way, there is a great need to understand how to increase literacy rates and educational success for students from generational poverty backgrounds," Beegle argues.

For instance, in 2008 the weekly earnings of high school dropouts were 27 percent less than those of high school graduates, 55 percent less than those of college graduates, 63 percent less than those of graduate school graduates, and 71 percent less than those of doctoral graduates. In addition, in 2010 high school dropouts were hit harder by joblessness during the recession, suffering unemployment rates of 14.7 percent in comparison with 10.6 percent for high school graduates and 4.7 percent for college graduates. "Lacking a high school diploma, these individuals will be far more likely than graduates to spend their lives periodically unemployed, on government assistance, or cycling in and out of the prison system,"[2] claims the Alliance of Excellent Education.

However, Kay Ann Taylor, associate professor of curriculum and instruction at Kansas State University, argues that the public education system contributes to poverty: "Rather than providing a venue for intellectual challenge, curiosity, and growth, too many of today's American public schools perpetuate ignorance in the form of dominant cultural reproduction that undermines independent thought and goes against the best interests of our students. These practices do not prepare students in American public schools to overcome or surpass conditions of poverty for themselves or society at large."[3] In addition, she points out that educators are ill equipped to deal with the particular challenges that poor youths face. "Teachers are placed in the forefront of this dilemma and many have no personal experience, much less idea or educational background to address issues of poverty in their classrooms in an understanding, empathetic, and caring manner," Taylor contends. In the following chapter, the authors present the main arguments for the causes of poverty in the world's wealthiest nation.

Notes

1. Donna M. Beegle, "Overcoming the Silence of Generational Poverty," *Talking Points*, October/November 2003.
2. Alliance for Excellent Education, "The High Cost of High School Dropouts: What the Nation Pays for Inadequate High Schools," *Issue Brief*, November 2011. www.all4ed.org.
3. Kay Ann Taylor, "Poverty's Multiple Dimensions," *Journal of Educational Controversy*, vol. 4, no. 1, Winter 2009.

"*The children of illegal aliens and foreign-born children of legal immigrants are nearly twice as likely to live in poverty.*"

Immigration Is Increasing Poverty in the United States

Eric A. Ruark and Matthew Graham

Eric A. Ruark is director of research at the Federation for American Immigration Reform (FAIR), where Matthew Graham is a staff member. In the following viewpoint, Ruark and Graham write that unchecked immigration contributes to poverty in the United States. The authors assert that the vast majority of immigrants are not admitted to the country based on skill or education, thereby saturating the labor market with unskilled workers. This displaces native workers and allows employers to offer low wages and dire conditions, they insist. Moreover, Ruark and Graham claim, unskilled immigrant households disproportionately use limited public resources and welfare programs, straining state and federal budgets.

As you read, consider the following questions:

1. How do Ruark and Graham back their position that immigrant populations are less educated compared to native-born citizens?

2. How do the authors counter the claim that immigrant workers take jobs native workers are unwilling or unable to do?

3. What percentage of immigrant households used welfare programs in 2007, as stated by the authors?

Immigration policy's effect on the labor force should be carefully considered, but the vast majority of immigrants are not admitted based on education or skill level. In 2009, the U.S. admitted over 1.1 million legal immigrants, just 5–8 percent of whom possessed employment skills in demand in the United States. By contrast, 66.1 percent were based on family preferences, or 73 percent if the relatives of immigrants arriving on employment visas are included. 16.7 percent of admissions were divided among refugees, asylum seekers and other humanitarian categories, while 4.2 percent of admissions were based on the diversity lottery (which only requires that winners have completed high school). Some family-based immigrants may be highly educated or skilled, but the vast majority of admissions are made without regard for those criteria.

The immigrant population reflects the system's lack of emphasis on skill. Nearly 31 percent of foreign-born residents over the age of 25 are without a high school diploma, compared to just 10 percent of native-born citizens. Immigrants trail natives in rates of college attendance, associate's degrees, and bachelor's degrees, but earn advanced degrees at a slightly higher rate (10.9 percent, compared to 10.4 percent for natives). Illegal immigrants are the least-educated group, with nearly 75 percent having at most a high school education.

Overall, 55 percent of the foreign-born population has no education past high school, compared to 42 percent of natives.

The median immigrant worker has an income of $30,000 per year, trailing native workers by about 18 percent. At $22,500 per year, illegal aliens make even less than their legal counterparts. Though U.S.-born children of legal immigrants are no more likely to be in poverty than those in native households, the children of illegal aliens and foreign-born children of legal immigrants are nearly twice as likely to live in poverty.

Both legal and illegal immigrants lag significantly behind natives in rates of health insurance coverage. Just 14 percent of native adults were uninsured in 2008, compared to 24 percent of legal immigrants and 59 percent of illegal aliens. Children were even more disproportionately uninsured. These low rates of insurance come despite a higher use of Medicaid than native households, 24.4 percent versus 14.7 percent in 2007. Overall, immigrants and their children make up about one-third of the uninsured population.

Immigrants in the Labor Market

A common argument adopted by defenders of illegal immigration is that illegal aliens only take jobs that natives are unwilling or unable to do. In reality, immigrants and natives compete in the same industries, and no job is inherently an "immigrant job." Less than 1 percent of the Census Bureau's 465 civilian job categories have a majority immigrant workforce, meaning that most employees in stereotypically "immigrant occupations" like housekeeping, construction, grounds keeping, janitorial service, and taxi service are actually natives.

The U.S. economy is oversaturated with unskilled labor. In May 2010, the unemployment rate for high school dropouts reached 15 percent, compared to just 4.7 percent among those with a bachelor's degree. If one included workers who are employed part time for economic reasons or want a job but have given up looking, many more millions of unemployed or underemployed workers are added to that total. Based on this measure, economists Andrew Sum and Ishwar Khatiwada used Current Population Survey data to peg the underutilization rate of high school dropouts at 35 percent, compared to 21 percent for high school graduates, 10 percent for bachelor's recipients, and just 7 percent among advanced degree earners.

Wage data and occupational patterns also indicate an unskilled labor surplus. The lowest rates of underutilization were found to be in "professional and managerial jobs" like legal, computer, and math-related occupations. Low-skill jobs had by far the highest underutilization rates, with food preparation and service at 24.7 percent, building and grounds cleaning at 24.6 percent, and construction at 32.7 percent. Even before the current economic downturn, indicators revealed a surplus of unskilled labor, as real hourly wages declined by 22 percent among male high school dropouts between 1979 and 2007. For male high school graduates, the drop was 10 percent. Over the same period, real wages for college graduates rose by 23 percent.

The current economic slowdown has reduced labor demand and forced many out of work, making it more important than ever to address the unskilled labor surplus. The labor force participation rate dropped from 63 percent in 2007 to 58.5 percent in June 2010, even while the unemployment rate more than doubled. Job competition has also greatly increased since the onset of the recession. The number of job seekers per job increased from about 1.5 in April 2007 to 5.0 in April 2010, a figure that does not account for underemployed or discouraged workers.

Immigration policy and enforcement are two of the most important determinants of America's labor supply, and the U.S. immigration system continues to contribute to the unskilled labor surplus, while the federal government has consistently failed to enforce the laws prohibiting the employment of illegal workers. Between 2000 and 2007, immigration increased the supply of high school dropouts in the labor force by 14.4 percent, compared to just a 2 to 4 percent increase for groups with higher educational attainment. A large share of the increase in unskilled labor was caused by illegal entry—over the same period, an estimated four million illegal immigrants took up residence in the U.S., about two million of whom had no diploma and another million of whom had no education past high school.

The large influx of unskilled, sometimes desperate workers has allowed employers to offer low wages and deplorable conditions. Special interests have successfully promoted the myth that Americans refuse to do some jobs, but in truth, immigrants and natives work alongside one another in all low-skill occupations. Reducing low-skill immigration, especially illegal immigration, would tighten the labor market and force employers to increase wages and improve working conditions. . . .

Overall, there is a massive pool of unskilled natives that needs work. In May 2010, 7.1 million natives with a high school diploma or less were unemployed, another 3.1 million were not considered part of the labor force but reported wanting a job, and 2.7 million more were working part time for an economic reason. It would make no sense to grant permanent legal status and full job market access to millions of unskilled illegal alien workers at the expense of these 12.9 million natives, not to mention the millions more whose wages have been undercut by low-skill immigration. Politicians should not succumb to corporate America's addiction to ever-growing quantities of unskilled immigrant labor.

Impact on Poor Americans

Regardless of their views about the overall economic effect of immigration, almost all economists agree that poor native workers bear the brunt of its negative consequences. Foreign-

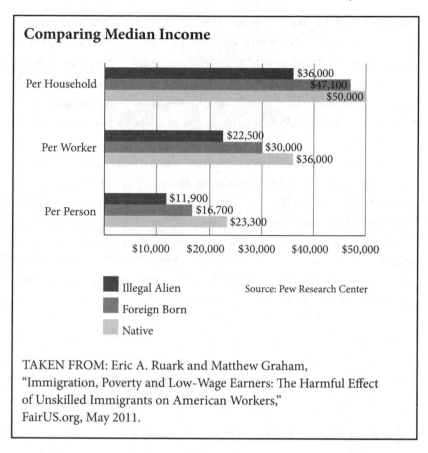

Comparing Median Income

TAKEN FROM: Eric A. Ruark and Matthew Graham,
"Immigration, Poverty and Low-Wage Earners: The Harmful Effect
of Unskilled Immigrants on American Workers,"
FairUS.org, May 2011.

born workers compete with natives on all skill levels, but because immigrants to the U.S. are disproportionately unskilled, they are especially likely to undercut the wages of low-skill natives. An analysis of America's 25 largest metropolitan areas showed that in high-skill industry groups like health professionals, technicians, administrative workers, and educators, immigrant earnings were usually within 10 percent of native wages; however, in unskilled groups like construction, machine operators, drivers, and farming, foreign-born workers consistently earned at least 10 percent less than their peers. Immigrant-native competition is an important concern in high-skill jobs, but is much more acute in low-skill industries.

Illegal aliens are the least skilled subset of the immigrant population, and therefore the most likely to undercut the wages and working conditions of low-skilled natives. Among seventeen industry categories named by the Pew Research Center as having the highest proportions of illegal aliens, data from the Current Population Survey reveal that noncitizens earned lower wages than natives in all but one of them. Data for noncitizens, which includes legal and illegal immigrants as well as temporary laborers, differ from data on illegal aliens because the latter tend to have lower wages and fewer skills. However, data on noncitizens are a much better fit for illegal aliens than using the foreign-born population as a whole. In construction, noncitizens earned less than two-thirds of natives' wage salaries, and in the two agricultural categories, they earned less than half. Wage and salary differences demonstrate how illegal and unskilled immigrants place downward pressure on wages by providing an incentive for employers to choose them over natives. The opportunity to exploit workers is the reason big business clamors for more immigrant labor. . . .

Jobs Americans Won't Do?

Related to the claim that there are not enough native workers is the assertion that Americans are unwilling to do certain types of work. In fact, the overabundance of unskilled labor is what allows employers to offer the poor conditions and low wages that make those jobs unattractive. In recent studies, some economists have advanced the idea that immigrants and natives cannot substitute for one another—in other words, that they take separate jobs in separate sectors and do not compete with one another. Unfortunately, the studies that advance the myth of "jobs Americans won't do" are rife with methodological errors. A careful examination of existing research and economic data demonstrates that natives and immigrants compete for the same jobs, and that immigrants reduce native wages.

The question of whether natives and immigrants can replace one another in the labor force is one of the most important factors in determining the effect of immigration on native wages and the labor market. Unfortunately, some economists have promoted the idea that immigrants only take jobs that natives are unwilling to do. Based on the critical assumption that immigrants and natives rarely compete with one another, Gianmarco Ottaviano and Giovanni Peri's oft-cited 2006 model found a 19.6 percent decline in earlier immigrants' wages due to immigration, compared to a 1.8 percent rise in native wages. The importance of the substitution question is difficult to overstate—economists that incorrectly assume a lack of substitutability between immigrants and natives conclude that immigration increases the value of native labor rather than creating competition. This helps create the illusion that immigration is a free lunch.

The idea that immigrants and natives cannot be substituted for one another does not hold up to scrutiny. No job is inherently an "immigrant job"—instead, employers make a conscious decision about what type of workers to use and the pay and conditions they offer. California's lemon industry made such exclusive use of Mexican migration networks and discriminatory hiring practices that it became nearly impossible for non-Hispanics to gain employment. The same was true of janitorial services in Los Angeles. The meatpacking industry, which once paid middle-class wages, has shifted to a low-wage rural factory model that makes heavy use of illegal workers. Meat producers have engaged in elaborate hiring schemes to bring thousands of illegal workers onto their payrolls, as have restaurants, hotels, construction companies, and producers in many other industries. The competitive advantage gained by the lawbreaker puts immense pressure on other producers to cut wages in order to stay competitive, even if they do not choose to break the law themselves.

It should be understood that these are shifts in employment practices, not a reaction to a permanent shortage of native workers. In the short run, individual job openings can become "immigrant jobs" without fundamentally changing natives' ability or willingness to do the work. However, if employers were not able to employ illegal aliens, common business practices would lead employers to increase wages and hire underutilized natives, just as they have adjusted their business models to take advantage of the current unskilled labor surplus. In recent years, immigrant labor has absorbed many job opportunities that previously went to unskilled natives. Within the unskilled labor force (high school education or less), the share of immigrants increased by 3.4 percent from 2000–05 as labor force participation among native unskilled workers fell by 4.1 percent. The drop in labor force participation was highest among unskilled workers aged 18 to 44.

It would be wrong to assume that literally every job position would be preserved if illegal workers vacated the labor market. In some cases, jobs would be automated or outsourced, and the decline in population would cause the economy to shrink slightly. However, given the low purchasing power of illegal aliens, the large costs borne by workers and taxpayers, the small predicted effect on prices, and the impossibility of outsourcing many jobs, average Americans would enjoy greater prosperity and have many more job opportunities available to them. In 2008, 8.3 million illegal aliens held jobs, but their economic impact only supported 2.8 million jobs. . . .

An Unnecessary Burden

The expansion of welfare programs is another cost of importing an excess of low-skill workers. It is difficult to justify the additional burden on limited public resources caused by immigrant-headed households whose admission contributes to the unskilled labor surplus. In 2004, the average unskilled immigrant household used $19,588 more in government services than it paid in taxes (an $8,836 gap at the federal level and $10,753 from state and local budgets). Illegal aliens impose a fiscal burden to state, local, and federal governments of an estimated $113 billion per year, but are the source of just $13 billion in tax revenue.

In 2007, 33 percent of immigrant-headed households used a major welfare program, compared to 19 percent of native-headed households. Further research has shown that in 2009, 57 percent of immigrant-headed households with children used at least one welfare program (39% native-headed). An estimated 40 percent of illegal alien households access welfare programs, often through their U.S.-born children. The usage gap between the immigrant and native populations can be largely, though not entirely, explained by their education level. An analysis of the four major education groups (less than high school, high school only, some college, and college graduates) found immigrant welfare use to be higher than their native counterparts at each level.

Immigrants who were admitted legally to the U.S. before the 1996 welfare reforms were subject to fewer legal restrictions on access to welfare programs. Use of food stamps and cash assistance was reduced by the reforms, but other programs, like the far more expensive Medicaid, drove immigrant welfare use rates past their pre-reform level in 2001 after falling in the late 1990s. With the exception of refugees, [asylum seekers], and the disabled, legal immigrant adults must wait five years to be eligible for food stamps, and may also receive TANF [Temporary Assistance for Needy Families] and Medicaid at their state's discretion after the waiting period. Immigrant children are eligible for food assistance immediately. After ten years of work history, legal immigrants become eligible for the full range of programs. In 2007, immigrants admitted during the previous seven years used welfare at a higher rate than the foreign-born population as a whole. Illegal immigrants are prohibited from accessing almost all programs, with exceptions for emergency medical assistance and a few other vital services that are not distributed based on economic need. However, they can still access the system through their U.S.-born children and by fraudulent means. . . .

Reforms to deter illegal immigration and to establish congruence in legal immigration between admission policy and the need for foreign workers are long overdue. A legal foreign worker admission policy in the national interest must take into consideration the flow of illegal aliens as well as guest workers and immigrant workers. It obviously would be unfair to continue to allow illegal aliens to supplant access of employers to legal foreign workers, so stemming the flow of illegal workers must be the first priority.

| "The inflow of low-skilled immigrants may even be playing a positive role in pushing native-born Americans up the skills and income ladder."

Immigration Is Not Increasing Poverty in the United States

Daniel Griswold

Daniel Griswold is the director of the Center for Trade Policy Studies at the Cato Institute. In the following viewpoint, the author contends that social and economic trends debunk the argument that the influx of low-skilled immigrants into the United States increases poverty. On the contrary, Griswold suggests, the American underclass has not grown with immigration. In addition, the arrival of low-skilled immigrants actually encourages native-born citizens to obtain higher education and skills, he persists, and—while driving some wages down—spurs economic growth that creates openings for higher-paid jobs. Overall, immigration moves Americans up socially and economically, Griswold maintains.

As you read, consider the following questions:

1. How was the rise of immigrant households in poverty between 1995 and 2004 offset, as told by Griswold?

2. How does the author compare immigration today to a century ago?

3. What evidence does the author offer to bolster his claim that male illegal immigrants have a strong propensity to work?

One argument raised against expanded legal immigration has been that allowing more low-skilled foreign-born workers to enter the United States will swell the ranks of the underclass. The critics warn that by "importing poverty," immigration reform would bring in its wake rising rates of poverty, higher government welfare expenditures, and a rise in crime. The argument resonates with many Americans concerned about the expanding size of government and a perceived breakdown in social order.

As plausible as the argument sounds, it is not supported by the social and economic trends of the past 15 years. Even though the number of legal and illegal immigrants in the United States has risen strongly since the early 1990s, the size of the economic underclass has not. In fact, by several measures the number of Americans living on the bottom rungs of the economic ladder has been in a long-term decline, even as the number of immigrants continues to climb. Other indicators associated with the underclass, such as the crime rate, have also shown improvement. The inflow of low-skilled immigrants may even be playing a positive role in pushing native-born Americans up the skills and income ladder.

Measuring the Size and Composition of the Underclass

"Underclass" is not a precise term, but it is generally understood to mean those who live below or near the poverty line and who lack the education or jobs skills to join the middle class. If we define the underclass to be the number of people in the United States living below the poverty line, in households earning less than $25,000 a year or without a high school diploma, and then examine the changing size and composition of each of those categories by either race or citizenship status, a consistent pattern emerges.

By all three measures, the size of the underclass has been shrinking since the early 1990s—during a period of large-scale legal and illegal immigration. The composition of the underclass has also been changing, with the number of immigrants and Hispanics growing, while the number of native-born and non-Hispanics has declined at an even more rapid rate.

Families and Individuals Below the Poverty Level. If we define the underclass as families living below the official poverty level, the recent trend has been downward. Between 1995 and 2004, the number of family households living below the poverty level fell by half a million, from 8.1 million to 7.6 million. The number of immigrant households in poverty did indeed rise—by 194,000—but that increase was more than offset by a drop of 675,000 in native-born households living in poverty. In other words, for every poor immigrant family we "imported" during that time, more than three native-born families were "exported" from poverty.

Poverty figures by race span a longer period, 1993 through 2007, but they tell the same story. The total number of family households living in poverty fell by 770,000 during that period, from 8.4 million to 7.6 million. The number of Hispanic families living in poverty increased by 420,000—providing evidence of a growing Hispanic/immigrant underclass—but over those same years, the number of non-Hispanic families in poverty dropped by 1.1 million, including a decline of 408,000 in the number of poor black families.

The trend is no different when we look at individuals in poverty. From 1993 through 2007, the number of individuals in our society subsisting below the poverty line declined by 2 million, from 39.3 million to 37.3 million. A 1.8 million increase in the number of Hispanics living in poverty was swamped by a 3.8 million decline in non-Hispanics, including a 1.6 million decline in black poverty. Similarly, a 1 million increase in immigrants living in poverty was more than matched by a 3 million drop in native-born Americans under the poverty line. Measured by the official poverty numbers, the American underclass has been shrinking as it has become composed of more immigrants and more Hispanics.

Households with Income Less than $25,000. Measuring the underclass by household income reveals the same underlying trend. The number of households earning less than $25,000 in a given year dropped by 5.6 million from 1995 to 2004, according to the most recent numbers that disaggregate the underclass by citizenship status. Almost all the drop was accounted for by a decline in nonimmigrant households earning less than $25,000, which dropped from 20.6 million in 1995 to 15.0 million in 2004. (All incomes were measured in inflation-adjusted dollars.) The number of immigrant families under that income threshold also dropped, but only by 80,000. As a result, the immigrant share of the underclass grew from 15 percent to 20 percent, even as the size of the underclass was shrinking.

The same picture emerges when we examine the number of low-income households by race and ethnicity. From 1994 through 2007, the number of households in America getting by on less than $25,000 fell by almost 10 million (with incomes measured across the years in real dollars). The share of total households living under that threshold dropped from 40 percent to 25 percent. Again, the entire decline was accounted for by non-Hispanic households, including a drop of 900,000 in black households, while the number of Hispanic households surviving on less than $25,000 was virtually unchanged.

Although the underclass became increasingly more Hispanic during the period, the share of all households living on less than $25,000 fell for every ethnic group. In fact, the steepest decline in percentage terms was among Hispanic households, with the share of households living below $25,000 dropping from 53 percent to 31 percent.

Householders and Individuals Without a High School Diploma. A third way of measuring the underclass is by householders or individuals without a high school diploma. In America today, a worker or head of household without a high school education is almost invariably confined to lower productivity, and thus, lower-wage occupations, with limited prospects for advancement.

As with the poverty and income measures, here, too, the story is basically positive. Between 1993 and 2006, the number of households headed by someone 18 and older without a high school diploma dropped by 3.7 million, from 19.9 million to 16.2 million. The number of such "low-skilled households" headed by a Hispanic did indeed increase by 1.8 million during that period, undoubtedly driven in significant part by large inflows of low-skilled immigrants from Mexico and Central America. The rest of the story, however, is that during those same years, the number of non-Hispanic households headed by a high school dropout fell by a hefty 5.5 million. That means that for every net addition of one Hispanic-headed, low-skilled household to the ranks of the underclass, the number of such non-Hispanic households dropped by three. Meanwhile, the share of total U.S. households headed by a high school dropout declined steadily, from one in five to one in seven. . . .

Educational attainment by citizenship status covers a slightly different period but also confirms the trend. From 1995 to 2004, the number of adults without a high school diploma declined by 2.9 million. An increase of 2.4 million in the number of immigrant dropouts was overwhelmed by a decline of 5.3 million in native-born dropouts. As that measure of the underclass shrank, the share represented by immigrants grew from 22 percent to 32 percent. By this and the other measures above, "the underclass" in our society has been shrinking as its face has become more Hispanic and foreign-born.

Immigrants Move In, Americans Move Up

Multiple causes lie behind the shrinking of the underclass in the past 15 years. The single biggest factor is probably economic growth. Despite the current recession, the U.S. economy enjoyed healthy growth during most of the period, lifting median household incomes and real compensation earned by U.S. workers, which ushered millions of families into the middle class and beyond. Welfare reform in the 1990s and rising levels of education may also be contributing factors.

Another factor may be immigration itself. The arrival of low-skilled, foreign-born workers in the labor force increases the incentives for younger native-born Americans to stay in school and for older workers to upgrade their skills. Because they compete directly with the lowest-skilled Americans, low-skilled immigrants do exert mild downward pressure on the wages of the lowest-paid American workers. But the addition of low-skilled immigrants also expands the size of the overall economy, creating openings in higher-paid occupations such as managers, skilled craftsmen, and accountants. The result is a greater financial reward for finishing high school and for acquiring additional job skills. Immigration of low-skilled workers motivates Americans, who might otherwise languish in the underclass, to acquire the education and skills necessary so they are not competing directly with foreign-born workers.

The shrinking of the native-born underclass contradicts the argument that low-skilled immigration is particularly harmful to African Americans, who are disproportionately represented in the underclass. By each of the three measures above—poverty, income, and educational attainment—the number of black American households and individuals in the underclass has been declining. Native-born blacks have been moving up along with other native-born Americans as immigrants have been moving in.

That same win-win dynamic may have been at work a century ago during the "great migration" of immigrants from eastern and southern Europe. Most of those immigrants were lower skilled compared with Americans, and their influx also exerted downward pressure on the wages of lower-skilled Americans. It was probably not a coincidence that during that same period the number of Americans staying in school to earn a high school diploma increased dramatically in what is called "the high school movement." From 1910 to 1940, the share of American 18-year-olds graduating from high school rose from less than 10 percent to 50 percent in a generation. Today's immigrants are arguably contributing to the same positive dynamic.

America's experience with immigration contradicts the simplistic argument that the arrival of a certain number of low-skilled immigrants increases the underclass by that very same amount. That approach ignores the dynamic and positive effects of immigration on native-born American workers. The common calculation that every low-skilled immigrant simply adds to the underclass betrays a static and inaccurate view of American society.

A Less Dysfunctional Underclass

Another contribution of immigration has been that it has changed the character of the American underclass for the better. Years of low-skilled immigration have created an underclass that is not only smaller than it was 15 years ago, but also more functional. Members of today's more immigrant and Hispanic underclass are more likely to work and less likely to live in poverty or commit crimes than members of the more native-born underclass of past decades.

One striking fact about low-skilled immigrants in America, both legal and illegal, is their propensity to work. In 2008, the labor-force participation rate of foreign-born Hispanics was 70.7 percent—compared to an overall rate of 65.6 percent for native-born Americans. Immigrants 25 years of age or older, without a high school diploma, were half again more likely to be participating in the labor force than native-born dropouts (61.1 percent vs. 38.4 percent). According to estimates by the Pew Hispanic Center, male illegal immigrants, ages 18–64, had a labor force participation rate in 2004 of an incredible 92 percent. Illegal immigrants are typically poor, but they are almost all working poor.

Nowhere is the contrast between the immigrant and native-born underclass more striking than in their propensity to commit crimes. Across all ethnicities and educational levels, immigrants are less prone to commit crimes and land in prison than their native-born counterparts.

The reasons behind this phenomenon are several. Legal immigrants can be screened for criminal records, reducing the odds that they will engage in criminal behavior once in the United States. Illegal immigrants have the incentive to avoid committing crimes to minimize their chances of being caught and deported. Legal or illegal, immigrants come to America to realize the opportunities of working in a more free-market, open, and prosperous economy; committing a crime puts that opportunity in jeopardy. . . .

Ironically, illegal immigrants who break U.S. immigration laws to enter the United States appear much more likely than native-born Americans to respect our domestic criminal code once they are inside the country. Once here, low-skilled immigrants, as a rule, get down to the business of earning money, sending home remittances, and staying out of trouble. The wider benefit to our society is that, in comparison to 15 years ago, a member of today's underclass, standing on a street corner, is more likely to be waiting for a job than a drug deal.

Contrary to popular notions, low-skilled immigration has not contributed to a swelling of the underclass, or any increase at all, nor has it contributed to a rise in crime or other antisocial behaviors. In fact, it would be more plausible to argue that low-skilled immigration has actually accelerated the upward mobility of Americans on the lower end of the socioeconomic ladder. At the same time, the influx of low-skilled immigrants has helped to transform the American underclass into a demographic group that is still poor—but more inclined to work and less prone to crime.

> *"Poverty in America, that true story goes, results from the choices that people make, not our economic system's supposed shortcomings."*

People Are Poor Through Their Own Bad Choices

Steven Malanga

In the following viewpoint, Steven Malanga maintains that people become poor due to their own actions, not the economy. He points out that women who choose to have children out of wedlock and not work full-time make up the overwhelming majority of poor households in New York City. Dropping out of high school is also a strong determinant, an unwise decision of many single parents that practically guarantees poverty, the author states. Malanga is a contributing editor to City Journal *and a senior fellow at the Manhattan Institute for Policy Research, a conservative think tank.*

As you read, consider the following questions:

1. How do the incomes of female-headed households compare to those of married couples in New York City, as described by the author?

2. What do left-wing critics argue about wages, as claimed by the author?

3. In Malanga's view, what advice do sociologists offer to stay out of poverty?

The release of the U.S. Census Bureau's mid-decade look at the population late last year [2006] sparked the usual outpouring of misinformed reporting on poverty. The familiar story line charged that our economic system isn't working well. The evidence? The poor are getting poorer, as one headline had it, and poverty rates remained unchanged, as another declared. In an editorial headlined "Downward Mobility," the *New York Times* explained that the [George W.] Bush agenda, emphasizing tax cuts and economic growth, wasn't adequate for helping the poor, who need a wide range of government interventions, from a higher minimum wage and a more progressive income tax to undefined "labor protections."

But the very same census study that provoked these headlines—the "American Community Survey" (ACS)—also reveals the true nature of much poverty in America, telling a story that the press either ignores or can't bring itself to write. Poverty in America, that true story goes, results from the choices that people make, not our economic system's supposed shortcomings.

The census's profile of poverty is especially revealing in a city like New York. With its wealthy families living side by side with a larger-than-average number of the poor, Gotham often appears in press accounts as a damning example of our society's inequities. The census's latest numbers tell us that the city's poverty rate is 19 percent, a number that hasn't changed much in 25 years and compares unfavorably with a national rate of about 13 percent. Places in New York—Manhattan, above all—seem the embodiment of former vice presidential candidate John Edwards's "Two Americas," with both a poverty rate and an average household income higher than the national average.

Disparities in Social Behavior

Yet behind the differences in economic performance of the "Two New Yorks" lie startling disparities in social behavior, usually unacknowledged by critics of our economic system. For instance, the latest ACS tells us that single parents head more than two-thirds of all of New York's poor families, including more than 183,000 run by single women. The median family income of female-headed households with children is just $21,233 annually, a stark contrast with the nearly $65,000 brought home by married couples with kids in New York. (Married couples are nearly two-thirds of all families not in poverty in the city.) In fact, economists from the University of California at Davis found in a recent study on poverty in America that "changes in family structure—notably a doubling of the percent of families headed by a single woman—can account for a 3.7 percentage point increase in poverty rates, more than the entire rise in the poverty rate from 10.7 percent to 12.8 percent since 1980."

It's not that the adults who head families in poverty don't earn enough; they don't work enough. Left-wing critics often charge that nowadays "work doesn't work" in our "broken" economic system, by which they mean that wages are so wretched that the poor can't lift themselves up, even when employed. But the ACS informs us that an adult working full-time heads up fewer than 16 percent of all impoverished New York households (and just slightly more than 16 percent nationwide). Among single-woman-headed households, just 14 percent work full-time; 55 percent don't work at all.

True, it may be hard to work full-time as a single mother unless you can afford child care. Yet in New York, ever more women—especially poor women—are choosing to have kids without a husband. The census shows that about 36,000 women annually in New York are now having children out of wedlock. That's one-third of all births in the city, though the data vary widely by race, with Asian Americans having the lowest out-of-wedlock rate (8 percent) and blacks the highest (62 percent). Most shocking, perhaps, is that more than half of women having children out of wedlock are already in poverty or wind up there within a year of giving birth. Those births to poor women partly explain the city's higher-than-average poverty rate; since the city's illegitimacy rate is above the nation's, a greater percentage of children are born directly into poverty here than nationwide.

Education, or the Lack of It

The second great demographic characteristic of poverty today is education, or the lack of it. The ranks of the impoverished overflow with high school dropouts, who are at a great disadvantage anywhere in America but above all in New York City, whose knowledge-based economy increasingly demands a sheepskin. In New York, almost seven in ten high school dropouts live in poverty, the ACS reports, compared with 40 percent of dropouts nationally. Many of those Gotham dropouts are also single parents, a double whammy that practically ensures poverty for themselves and their children.

The importance of at least a high school diploma for success in America also helps explain why Gotham's higher-than-average immigration rate worsens the city's poverty. New York has a far greater stream of foreign-born residents arriving each year, relative to its population, than does the United States as a whole. And 27 percent come without even a high school education. No surprise then, as the ACS shows, that 30 percent of all recent immigrants are poor (though less so than back home)—an average of about 23,000 new recruits to the ranks of the city's poor every year.

New York City also seems to be a magnet for the poor from elsewhere in the U.S., perhaps because of the lavish housing and welfare benefits that it offers. About 14 percent of those who've crossed state lines to move to Gotham—domestic immigrants, the census calls them—are poor, too, an unusually high poverty rate for such immigrants. The result is that almost exactly half of New York City's poor are born somewhere else—either overseas or in another state. The city, in other words, imports much of its poverty. Given these trends, it's remarkable that the city's poverty rate is stable, not soaring.

Sociologists will point out (at least in their candid moments) that most people can stay out of poverty in America by doing just a few simple things—most importantly, graduating from high school and not having kids without a spouse on hand. The latest census survey reinforces this basic wisdom. Sooner or later, the press will get it.

> "Despite projections about a slow but steady economic turnaround, economists say this recession will leave deep scars beneath the surface—especially for those who were already struggling."

Job Loss Due to the Recession Is Increasing Poverty

Claudia Rowe

In the following viewpoint, Claudia Rowe states that the recent recession has resulted in job losses and instability, pushing many middle-class families into poverty. Unemployment rates have reached historic highs, she claims, and the numbers of unemployed college students have tripled from 2007 to 2010. Persisting that low-income and minority households are among the hardest hit, Rowe questions what policies or systems hold economic opportunities from these groups. The author is a contributor to Equal Voice, *a newspaper that focuses on poor families, and an award-winning journalist who has worked for the* New York Times *and* Seattle Post-Intelligencer.

As you read, consider the following questions:

1. What percentage of American families has been affected by job loss, reduced work hours, or a pay cut, as claimed by Rowe?

2. In the author's view, what factors required to transcend economic class have been stunted by the recession?

3. As described by Rowe, what does the federal government consider a low-income household?

In America, where we celebrate success above all, the worst thing a person can be is poor.

For much of her adult life, Tinsa Hall felt like she had it made, at least relative to where she'd been. She lived in a six-bedroom home on a wide, tree-lined street in a solidly middle-class neighborhood. Her husband fixed computers for a living. They had three healthy children, and Hall, who'd had some difficulty with her own academic career, attended every school board meeting she could, vowing that her kids would get a better start in life than she. Until last year [in 2009], that appeared to be the case.

But things have changed. Hall, 36, now lives in a squat, dark rental on the other side of town, where the sidewalk is jagged and the streets are pocked with holes. Her grand old home was gutted by fire last spring, and her marriage was in tatters months before that. She supports her family on $19,080 a year—poverty-level wages, according to the federal government—earned training local youth in alternatives to violence. Often, the job keeps her late into the evening, meaning that her teenage son and two daughters are on their own for dinner.

Hall, however, is glad to have the work. Unemployment in her home state, Mississippi, is over 14 percent for African Americans, and with no college degree, she sees little opportunity to earn more. Rent eats up a third of her monthly income, and after utility bills, food, her car payment and gas, there is nothing left to save. "I feel like I'm starting all over again," she said.

Though the split with her husband touched off Hall's economic plunge, the broad outlines of her financial crisis are now shared by millions—more each month as figures tracking home foreclosures, food stamp use and unemployment continue to hover at rates not seen since the Great Depression of the 1930s.

Since 2008, about 44 percent of American families have experienced a job loss, reduction in hours or pay cut. Nearly 15 million adults are currently unemployed, and even without the most recent data from 2009, 14 million children, like Hall's, were growing up in poverty. Rather than being publicly labeled as "reduced-lunch kids" in front of their friends, many prefer to leave school hungry.

The Transformed American Economy

Over the coming months, *Equal Voice* will talk with families about what this transformed American economy means to their daily lives. Funded by the Marguerite Casey Foundation, which supports organizations in the nation's poorest regions, we will report on the ways government policy affects parents and children from the Mississippi Delta to greater Los Angeles, inner-city Chicago to the Mexican border states and Appalachia. We aim to address the ramifications of increased poverty among those who have struggled for generations, as well as for the millions of new poor.

"Simply put, poverty is not good for the economy," said John S. Irons, research and policy director at the Economic Policy Institute. When children grow up poor, they have higher dropout rates, less education overall and vastly diminished job prospects. Some economists estimate that childhood poverty costs Americans about $500 billion per year in lost productivity and increased spending on health care and criminal justice.

Hall may not have those numbers at her fingertips, but she is well aware of the overall trend. As president of the Greenville High School Parent Teacher Association [PTA] and a member of the statewide PTA board, she routinely lobbies for children in the all-black Greenville public schools when officials might prefer to treat them as percentiles. Proudly, she displays her son's and daughters' academic trophies. Now she wonders whether any of it will matter. "You got kids who are coming out of college with degrees and can't find a job, so college—for what?" she said, nervously rubbing her hands up and down her legs.

Indeed, in March 2010, there were 2.3 million unemployed college graduates, almost triple the number looking for work three years ago.

Although it is no secret that family wealth shapes opportunity—financing an education, say, or startup costs for a new business—less known is the fact that 13 percent of white households had zero net worth in 2004. More than 29 percent of black households were in that category.

The Recession's Deep Scars

Despite projections about a slow but steady economic turnaround, economists say this recession will leave deep scars beneath the surface—especially for those who were already struggling. Irons, of the Economic Policy Institute, believes crushed education and employment opportunities will affect "the future prospects of all family members—including children—and will have consequences for years to come."

Yet the American Dream is built on the concept of upward mobility, the notion that families can leave poverty behind if they simply work hard enough. The corresponding belief—that the poor are poor due to their own bad choices—resounds through our society. Yet research showing that 45 percent of children who grow up in poverty remain poor as adults suggests this may be myth more than reality.

"When you have high inequality combined with low mobility then you have a country that is not the America that we think of, a country of opportunity," said Heidi Shierholz, an economist who specializes in policy affecting low-wage workers. "That's not the American promise."

Even in good times, the ability to transcend class depends on a complex constellation of factors—the right education, job opportunities, role models and, not least, a child's aspirations—all of them potentially stunted by economic tremors like those of the past two years. As of last fall one in seven mortgages was delinquent, and by Christmas foreclosure notices had gone out to nearly 3 million people. Some economists predict that another 5 million families could lose their homes this year.

Those are not only homeowners who have hit rock bottom. One out of every three families with children are getting by on less than $44,000 a year, which the federal government considers "low income." Some 29 million kids fall into that category.

One of them is Alexis Walker, 17, who lives in Long Beach, Calif., with her mother, older sister and 5-year-old nephew. Each day at 2 a.m., Ursula Walker leaves for her $20-an-hour job as a mail sorter. She never knows how much the postal service will have her work in a day—three hours, four, eight?— which means Ursula is never sure how much she'll earn. All she knows is that overtime has vanished during the last year and her regular hours keep dwindling. To help, Alexis buys school clothes with a community center stipend.

"I don't know what's in between barely surviving and middle-income, but we're there," Alexis said. "People like us, we get overlooked a lot."

Through this series, *Equal Voice* seeks to address several questions: How exactly do we define poverty as individuals and as a country? Perhaps more important, how do the poor see themselves? What systems or policies—despite current federal action—bar groups of people from economic opportunity, and how does one child claw her way out while another is crushed? Most of all, what lessons can we take from the past about the best ways to address what is surely a new wave of American poor in the making?

Periodical and Internet Sources Bibliography

The following articles have been selected to supplement the diverse views presented in this chapter.

Janel Davis	"Single Mothers Struggle to Stay Out of Poverty," *Gazette* (Gaithersburg, MD), June 17, 2009.
Shaila Dewan	"A Racial Divide Is Bridged by Recession," *New York Times*, November 16, 2009. www.nytimes.com.
John Flynn	"Poverty—The High Cost of Marriage Breakdown," Catholics for the Common Good, September 26, 2010. http://.ccgaction.org.
Jacob G. Hornberger	"The Cause of Poverty," *Hornberger's Blog*, Future of Freedom Foundation, March 12, 2009. www.fff.org.
Chris L. Jenkins	"Hard Times: Half the Income, All the Responsibility," *Washington Post*, November 10, 2010. www.washingtonpost.com.
Judith Morrison	"Race and Poverty in Latin America: Addressing the Development Needs of African Descendants," *UN Chronicle*, September 2007.
Steven Raphael and Eugene Smolensky	"Immigration and Poverty in the United States," *Focus*, Fall 2009.
William Rodgers III	"Understanding the Black-White Earnings Gap," *American Prospect*, September 22, 2008.
Anup Shah	"Corruption," Global Issues, September 4, 2011. www.globalissues.org.
Frosty Wooldridge	"Our Troubled Country: Importing Poverty," NewsWithViews.com, June 16, 2008. www.newswithviews.com.

OPPOSING
VIEWPOINTS®
SERIES

CHAPTER 3

How Can Poverty Be Reduced in the United States?

Chapter Preface

In 2010 unemployment insurance prevented 3.2 million job-less Americans from falling into poverty, according to the US Census Bureau. In 2009 it kept a record 3.3 million above the poverty line. These benefits "had a much bigger poverty-fighting impact in this recession than in the previous three recessions,"[1] asserts Arloc Sherman, a senior researcher at the Center on Budget and Policy Priorities. He states that the number of people receiving unemployment insurance jumped 2.8 million, or 581 percent, from 2007 to 2009. In contrast, in the recessions that occurred in 2001 and in the early 1990s, Sherman adds, that number never increased more than 1 million, or 209 percent.

As a federal program, unemployment insurance is widely praised in reducing poverty. "As heartbreaking as the census data is, it's worth remembering that government spending prevented it from being even worse,"[2] suggests Steven Benen, a political writer and blogger for the *Washington Monthly*. Others propose that these benefits boost the economy, which is especially valuable during a recession. "They provide the biggest bang for the buck of the various kinds of government spending,"[3] claim Heather Boushey and Matt Separa, a senior economist and a research assistant, respectively, at the Center for American Progress. "That spending helps boost local economies as the unemployed can continue to pay their mortgage or rent and put food on the table," they state.

Nonetheless, some commentators draw attention to the drawbacks of unemployment insurance. "Like any government stimulus, jobless benefits will eventually become a drag on the economy. The federal government should not subsidize two years of unemployment forever,"[4] insists Derek Thompson, an editor covering business for the *Atlantic*. Unemployment insurance fraud is also a major problem. In 2010 individuals who were ineligible or kept claiming unemployment after returning to work cashed in $17 billion in benefits. "This is a national concern,"[5] observes Raymond Filippone, assistant director of income support at the Rhode Island Department of Labor and Training. "States across the country are stepping up and looking at overpayments and detection," he explains. In the following chapter, the authors examine the policies, programs, and economics of fighting poverty.

Notes

1. Arloc Sherman, "Looking at Today's Poverty Numbers," *Off the Charts* (blog), Center on Budget and Policy Priorities, September 16, 2010. www.offthechartsblog.org.
2. Steven Benen, "Unemployment Insurance Keeps Millions Out of Poverty," *Political Animal* (blog), *Washington Monthly*, September 16, 2010. www.washingtonmonthly .com.
3. Heather Boushey and Matt Separa, "Unemployment Insurance Dollars Create Millions of Jobs," Center for American Progress, September 21, 2011. www.americanprogress.org.
4. Derek Thompson, "The Case For and Against Unemployment Insurance," *Atlantic*, July 20, 2010. www.theatlantic .com.
5. Associated Press, "States Crack Down on Unemployment Insurance Fraud," FOX News, July 4, 2010. www.foxnews .com.

> "Today, there is a great gap between the
> minimum wage and a minimum living
> standard."

Raising the Minimum Wage Will Reduce Poverty

Holly Sklar

Holly Sklar is director of Business for Shared Prosperity, senior policy advisor to the Let Justice Roll Living Wage Campaign, and a syndicated columnist. In the following viewpoint, she claims that increasing the minimum wage would lift workers and families out of poverty. According to the author, minimum wage has fallen far behind the cost of living; the raise of the federal minimum wage to $7.25 an hour in 2009 is still worth less than it was in the 1950s. Setting the minimum wage to $10 would adjust for inflation and provide a minimum standard of living for low-income working households, Sklar proposes.

As you read, consider the following questions:

1. What does setting the minimum wage too low mean, in Sklar's opinion?

2. How does Sklar respond to the position that raising the minimum wage would increase unemployment?

3. How does the budget for a one-parent, one-child household in 2007 provided by the Economic Policy Institute compare to that year's poverty threshold, as described by the author?

The decade between the federal minimum wage increase to $5.15 an hour on Sept. 1, 1997, and the July 24, 2007, increase to $5.85 was the longest period in history without a raise.

- Family health insurance, which cost half a year's minimum wage income in 1998, costs more than the total annual minimum wage today.

Recent minimum wage raises are so little, so late that even with the minimum wage increase on July 24, 2009, to $7.25, workers will still make less than they did in 1956, adjusting for the increased cost of living.

- The 1956 minimum wage is worth $7.93 in today's dollars.

We cannot build a strong 21st-century economy on 1950s wages.

Workers Have Taken Many Steps Back for Every Step Forward Since 1968

The minimum wage reached its peak value in 1968. It would take a $9.92 minimum wage today to match the buying power of the minimum wage in 1968—four decades ago.

- In 2009 dollars, the 1968 hourly minimum wage of $9.92 adds up to $20,634 a year.

- The July 24, 2009, minimum wage of $7.25 comes to just $15,080 a year.

The two longest periods without a minimum wage increase both occurred in recent decades (between the raises on Jan. 1, 1981, and Apr. 1, 1990, and between those on Sept. 1, 1997, and July 24, 2007). To make matters worse, the minimum wage increases after the record-breaking periods without a raise were small compared to prior increases over shorter time spans.

It is immoral that the minimum wage is worth less now than it was in 1968, the year Dr. Martin Luther King was killed in Memphis while fighting for living wages for sanitation workers—and all workers.

$10 in 2010 will bring the minimum wage closer to the value it had in 1968, a year when the unemployment rate was a low 3.6%. The next year, unemployment was 3.5%.

Minimum Wage Does Not Provide a Minimally Adequate Living Standard

The federal minimum wage was enacted in 1938 through the Fair Labor Standards Act [FLSA], designed to eliminate "labor conditions detrimental to the maintenance of the minimum standard of living necessary for health, efficiency and general well-being of workers."

When set too low, the minimum wage does the opposite of what the Fair Labor Standards Act intended by reinforcing detrimental labor conditions.

Setting minimum wage too low means people are continually juggling which necessities to go *without*. Will it be "heat or eat," rent or health care?

Setting minimum wage too low means more working people and families living in homeless shelters and cars. Setting minimum wage too low means more working people turning to overwhelmed food banks.

- According to the National Low Income Housing Coalition, there is no county in the country where a full-time worker making minimum wage can afford a one-bedroom apartment, (without spending more than 30% of their income on housing).

- The 2008 Conference of Mayors' Hunger and Homelessness Survey found that 42% of persons requesting emergency food assistance were employed, as were 19% of the homeless.

- In the words of the Mayors' report, "Philadelphia writes, 'new people coming to food cupboards are people that are employed with children. . . .' Gastonia, North Carolina, reported, 'We are seeing more two-parent households that are employed.' In Salt Lake City, the 'increased costs of housing, utilities, transportation and food force low-wage families to request food on a regular basis.'"

It is immoral that workers earning minimum wage, who care for children, the ill and the elderly, struggle to care for themselves and their families.

The Minimum Wage Is a Poverty Wage Instead of an Antipoverty Wage

You can't fight poverty with a poverty wage. Poverty rates are higher now than in the 1970s, thanks in part to the eroded value of the minimum wage.

Contrary to stereotype, the typical minimum wage worker is an adult over age 20. Most have high school degrees or beyond. They are health care aides who can't afford sick days, and child care workers, retail clerks and farm workers. They are hospitality workers without paid vacation and security guards turning to overwhelmed food banks to help feed their families.

They are young adults trying to work their way through college on wages that have fallen far behind the rising cost of tuition, housing, food and fees.

- Between 1978–79 and 2008–09, adjusting for inflation, tuition and fees at public four-year colleges rose 119%. The inflation-adjusted value of the minimum wage dropped about 25% in the same period.

A low minimum wage gives a green light to employers to pay poverty wages to a growing share of the workforce.

More jobs are keeping people in poverty instead of out of poverty. As the wage floor has dropped below poverty levels, millions of workers find themselves with paychecks above the minimum—but not above the poverty line. More and more workers are in jobs with low wages and little or no benefits. More children of working parents are growing up in poverty.

A Low Minimum Wage Institutionalizes an Increasingly Low-Wage Workforce

The minimum wage sets the wage floor. If the minimum wage had held the near-$10 value it had in 1968, it would have put upward pressure—rather than downward pressure—on the average worker wage.

If the minimum wage had held the near-$10 value it had in 1968, Wal-Mart and McDonald's, our nation's largest employers, couldn't routinely pay wages much lower.

- Wal-Mart's wages would be closer to Costco, which pays starting wages of $11 an hour plus much better benefits. Costco CEO Jim Sinegal has long asserted, *"Paying your employees well is not only the right thing to do, but it makes for good business."*

- McDonald's wages would be more like In-N-Out Burger, which has a starting wage of $10 an hour plus benefits and has long ranked first or second nationwide among fast-food chains in overall excellence.

Most of the ten occupations projected by the Bureau of Labor Statistics to have the largest employment growth during 2006–2016 have disproportionate numbers of minimum wage workers.

These include retail salespersons, fast-food workers, home health aides and janitors. Raising the minimum wage is essential to them, their families and our economy.

Workers Have Not Gotten "A Fair Day's Pay for a Fair Day's Work"

"As the productivity of workers increases, one would expect worker compensation to experience similar gains," a 2001 U.S. Department of Labor report observed. Workers used to share in the gains of rising worker productivity. In recent decades, worker productivity went up, but workers' wages went down. Increasingly, the gains have gone to owners and top executives.

- Between 1947 and 1973, worker productivity rose 104% and the minimum wage rose 101%, adjusted for inflation. The middle class grew.

- Between 1973 and 2008, productivity rose 87% and the minimum wage fell 16%, adjusted for inflation. Average worker wages fell 10%. The middle class shrunk.

Profits have gone up while worker wages have gone down.

- Between 1973 and 2008, domestic corporate profits rose 139%.

- Profits in the disproportionately low-wage retail industry increased even more: 187%.

Contrary to myth, higher education does not protect workers from falling real wages. Since 1973, the share of workers without a high school degree has plummeted and the percentage with at least four years of college has more than doubled. But the 2008 average hourly wage was 10% below 1973, adjusted for inflation.

- The inflation-adjusted wages of recent college graduates were lower in 2007 than in 2001.

A Low Minimum Wage Reinforces a Growing Gap Between Haves and Have-Nots

There has been a massive shift of income from the bottom and middle to the top. The richest 1% of Americans has increased their share of the nation's income to a higher level than any year since 1928—the eve of the Great Depression.

- In 1973, the richest 1% of Americans had 9% of national income. By 2006, they had 23%.

CEOs [chief executive officers] at big corporations make more in a couple hours than minimum wage workers make in a year—not counting CEO perks and benefits.

- In 1980, the average CEO at a big corporation made as much as 97 minimum wage workers.

- In 1997, the average CEO made as much as 728 minimum wage workers.

- In 2007—the last year of the longest period in history without a raise in the minimum wage—CEOs made as much as 1,131 minimum wage workers.

It is immoral that some are paid so little their children go without necessities—while others are paid so much their grandchildren will live in luxury without having to work at all.

The minimum wage is not just about fair pay for workers. It is an essential part of the foundation of our economy and society. We can't build a strong economy with a widening gap between the top and bottom any more than we can have a strong apartment building with an ever more luxurious penthouse at the top and a crumbling foundation below. . . .

Raising the Minimum Wage Does Not Increase Unemployment

Critics routinely oppose minimum wage increases in good times and bad, claiming they will increase unemployment, no matter the real-world record to the contrary. The buying power of the minimum wage reached its peak in 1968. The unemployment rate went from 3.8% in 1967 to 3.6% in 1968 to 3.5% in 1969.

The next time the unemployment rate came close to those levels was after the minimum wage raises of 1996 and 1997. Contrary to what critics predicted when the minimum wage was raised, our economy had unusually low unemployment, high growth, low inflation, and declining poverty rates between 1996 and 2000. The unemployment rate fell from 5.6% in 1995 to 4% in 2000. Unemployment went down across the board across the country—including among people of color, teenagers, high school graduates with no college, and those with less than a high school education.

As *Business Week* put it in 2001, "Many economists have backed away from the argument that minimum wage [laws] lead to fewer jobs."

States that raised their minimum wages above the long stagnant $5.15 federal level experienced better employment and small business trends than states that did not.

Recent studies by the Institute for Research on Labor and Employment (Univ. of CA, Berkeley), carefully controlling for non-minimum wage factors, further advance the extensive research, which shows that minimum wage raises do not cause increased unemployment. . . .

A Minimum of $10 in 2010 Is Needed for a Minimum Standard of Living

Original proposals for the Fair Labor Standards Act "provided for a commission that would set the minimum wage after a public hearing and consideration of cost-of-living estimates provided by the Bureau of Labor Statistics (BLS). By this procedure, the wage would have been updated according to changes in the standard of living and inflation. The version of the FLSA that became law, however, left action on future increases to Congress and the president."

Today, there is a great gap between the minimum wage and a minimum living standard.

In 2001, the *Raise the Floor[: Wages and Policies That Work for All of Us]* book and Ms. Foundation Raise the Floor project called for an $8 federal minimum wage based on a carefully researched *national average minimum needs budget* for a single adult (including housing, health care, food and other necessities, and taxes and tax credits). *Raise the Floor* research showed such a minimum wage would be not only affordable but also beneficial to business. A companion poll in 2002 found that

77% of likely voters favored increasing the minimum wage to $8 an hour. $8 in 2001 is worth $9.66 now.

The official poverty measure has become so out of touch with reality that research shows you need about double the official poverty threshold to get a more realistic measure of what people actually need to afford necessities.

- For example, according to the Economic Policy Institute's [EPI's] online Basic Family Budget Calculator, the national median basic needs budget (including taxes and tax credits) for a one-parent, one-child family was $30,761 in 2007 while the Census Bureau's 2007 poverty threshold for a one-parent, one-child family was $14,291.

According to the Economic Policy Institute, 30% of families have incomes less than adequate for a family budget meeting necessities. Among families with a full-time worker, 23% fall short of a Basic Family Budget. (EPI's data does not include single-person households.)

The minimum wage should be raised to $10 in 2010. That's a full-time annual wage income of $20,800.

Future minimum wage increases should reflect the updated cost of an adequate minimum living standard. We should not repeat the error of the poverty measure and lock in an eroded minimum wage by indexing it to inflation from an inadequate base level.

Adjusting for inflation means the minimum wage goes up as inflation goes up. It's like running in place instead of falling backwards. But it's not moving forward—sharing the gains of higher productivity and economic progress. It's not "A fair day's pay for a fair day's work." It does not strengthen the floor under our economy and society.

> "A higher minimum wage does not re-
> duce poverty rates, and because of the
> perverse way that many government
> aid programs are structured, it will also
> do little to help the neediest minimum-
> wage families."

Raising the Minimum Wage Will Not Reduce Poverty

James Sherk

In the following viewpoint, James Sherk maintains that increasing the minimum wage will not raise disadvantaged families and unskilled workers out of poverty. Most workers earning the minimum wage are high school and college students who do not support themselves, Sherk asserts, and most households below the poverty line do not work full-time. In fact, he suggests that an increase in the minimum wage will be counterproductive: It would eliminate the entry-level positions that are vital for unskilled workers to enter the workforce and cut off families from valuable government benefits. Sherk is a senior policy analyst in labor economics at the Heritage Foundation.

As you read, consider the following questions:

1. What evidence does the author provide to bolster his assertion that few minimum-wage earners support their families on their incomes?

2. How does raising the minimum wage to $7.25 an hour specifically affect workers receiving government benefits, in the author's view?

3. What did one study reveal about the long-term consequences of increasing the minimum wage, as told by Sherk?

Supporters of raising the federal minimum wage make a seemingly compelling argument when they point out that the minimum wage has not increased in almost a decade. During that time, they note, inflation has steadily eaten away at the purchasing power of a $5.15-per-hour wage. It seems only fair that the government should step in now and boost the earnings of America's lowest-paid workers.

Despite its proponents' good intentions, raising the minimum wage will not accomplish this goal and will have many unintended consequences.

Few of those who would benefit from a higher minimum wage are disadvantaged workers. Nor do minimum-wage workers need the government to step in for them to earn a raise. A higher minimum wage does not reduce poverty rates, and because of the perverse way that many government aid programs are structured, it will also do little to help the neediest minimum-wage families.

Raising the minimum wage has other unintended effects, however. For one thing, it causes businesses to hire fewer workers, and it particularly discourages businesses from hiring the least-skilled workers who most need assistance. Losing access to entry-level positions deprives many unskilled workers of the opportunity to learn the skills they need to advance up a career ladder. Thus, a minimum-wage hike harms these workers' job prospects for years after it takes effect.

Good intentions are not enough to make good policy, nor do they abolish the law of unintended consequences.

Who Earns the Minimum Wage?

Many people assume that most minimum-wage workers live in poverty, but this is not the case. Just a small minority of those earning the federal minimum wage—less than one in five—live at or below the poverty line. Why do so few minimum-wage workers live in poverty when a minimum-wage job is not enough to put a family of three above the poverty line?

Part of the answer is that few minimum-wage workers rely on their pay to support themselves. The average family income of a minimum-wage worker is $49,885 a year. Further, the majority of minimum-wage workers are between the ages of 16 and 24. These are high school and college students seeking to supplement their family's earnings, not to make it on their own. Similarly, more than three-fifths of all minimum-wage earners work only part-time.

In addition, very few minimum-wage earners support families on their income. Less than 1 in 25 minimum-wage workers are single parents who work full-time. Even among the minority of minimum-wage earners who are over the age of 24, and thus more likely to be parents, just 1 in 16 are single parents who work full-time—no different from the population as a whole. So while a minimum-wage job will not put a family of three over the poverty line, very few rely on minimum-wage jobs to do so.

Some minimum-wage workers do fit the stereotypes—for example, a single mother struggling to support her family on a meager income—but most do not. Because of the profile of those who earn the minimum wage, most of the benefits of increasing it would accrue to workers early in their careers who have limited family obligations.

The Problem Is Work, Not Wages

Few minimum-wage workers are from poor families. This poor worker stereotype does not cover the vast majority of minimum-wage workers. It is true, however, that a small number of workers without a realistic possibility of promotion are trying to support children on a minimum-wage income. Even if most of the benefits of a higher minimum wage go to other workers, would it still help particularly disadvantaged workers to get ahead?

No. Many economic studies show that raising the minimum wage does not lift workers out of poverty. If anything, it makes the problem of poverty worse. As one research paper explains, this effect is clear:

> The answer we obtain to the question of whether minimum wage increases reduce the proportion of poor and low-income families is a fairly resounding "no." The evidence on both family income distributions and changes in incomes experienced by families indicates that minimum wages raise the incomes of some poor families, but that their net effect is to increase the portion of families that are poor and near-poor.

The minimum wage does so little to reduce poverty because it does nothing to address the real problems behind poverty. Most poor Americans do not work for the minimum wage. In fact, most poor Americans do not work at all. . . .

[In 2005], only 11 percent of adults living below the poverty line worked full-time year-round, and more than three-fifths did not work at all. The median family with children living below the poverty line works only 1,040 hours a year in total—just 20 hours a week. Most of these families are poor because they do not work full-time, not because they earn low wages. If at least one parent in every poor household worked full-time year-round, the child poverty rate in the United States would plummet by 72 percent. Raising the minimum wage does not address this problem and so will not reduce poverty rates.

Government Programs Blunt the Minimum Wage's Impact

Additionally, even among those very few low-income workers who might receive a wage boost due to a higher minimum wage, few would benefit in terms of a higher standard of living.

Due to the perverse structure of many government anti-poverty programs, increases in the minimum wage do very little to help truly needy workers. While the minimum wage affects all low-skilled workers, the government has a vast array of programs directly targeted at low-income families. Programs like Temporary Assistance for Needy Families, Medicaid, child-care assistance, housing assistance, and food stamps provide low-income families with generous food, housing, child care, and medical benefits and direct income supplements. These programs ensure that a low-income family with only a minimum-wage income lives well above the poverty line even though minimum-wage earnings alone would leave the family below the line.

The problem is that these programs phase out as workers' earnings rise. For each dollar workers earn above a certain amount, they lose a portion of their benefits. Truly needy workers earning the minimum wage who qualify for many of these programs—for example, a single parent trying to raise a family—would lose almost as much in forgone government benefits as they would gain from a higher minimum wage. Raising the minimum wage to $7.25 an hour would increase minimum-wage workers' earnings by 41 percent. After adjust-

Harming How Workers Are Compensated

In addition to making jobs hard to find, minimum wage laws may also harm workers by changing how they are compensated. Fringe benefits—such as paid vacation, free room and board, inexpensive insurance, subsidized child care, and on-the-job training—are an important part of the total compensation package for many low-wage workers. When minimum wages rise, employers can control total compensation costs by cutting benefits. In extreme cases, employers convert low-wage full-time jobs with benefits to high-wage part-time jobs with no benefits and fewer hours.

Linda Gorman, "Minimum Wages,"
The Concise Encyclopedia of Economics,
Library of Economics and Liberty. www.econlib.org.

ing for lost benefits, however, these workers' total income, if they worked full-time, would rise only 3 percent to 5 percent in most states. In some states, like North Dakota, low-income families would actually be worse off than before.

The poorly conceived structure of the government's anti-poverty programs prevents a higher minimum wage from helping truly needy minimum-wage workers. Suburban high school students and college students who do not receive government assistance would enjoy somewhat higher earnings, but the heads of low-income families would not. What gains in higher wages these families received would be offset by reduced government benefits. And this assumes that needy workers would keep their jobs and not suffer reduced working hours due to a minimum-wage hike.

Workers *Earn* Raises

Another mistaken assumption is that minimum-wage workers' incomes will rise only if the government raises the minimum wage. In fact, few workers start at the minimum wage and then stay there for decades. Minimum-wage jobs are the first rung on a career ladder that soon leads to higher-paying jobs. Very few workers who earned the minimum wage a decade ago still earn it today.

This is because minimum-wage jobs are entry-level positions. Minimum-wage workers are typically low-skilled and have little workforce experience. Fully 40 percent of minimum-wage workers did not have a job the year before. Minimum-wage jobs teach these workers valuable job skills, such as how to interact with customers and coworkers or accept direction from a boss—expertise that is difficult to learn without actual on-the-job experience. Once workers have gained these skills, they become more productive and earn higher wages.

The evidence shows that minimum-wage workers quickly earn raises. Between 1998 and 2003—a time when the federal minimum wage did not rise—over two-thirds of workers starting out at the minimum wage earned more than that a year later. Once workers have gained the skills and experience that make them more productive, they can command higher wages.

Workers also have a say in how quickly they become more productive. Most minimum-wage earners work part-time, and many are students and young adults who desire this flexibility. But minimum-wage workers who choose to work longer hours gain more skills and experience than those who work part-time and, as expected, earn larger raises. A typical minimum-wage employee who works 35 hours or more a week is 13 percent more likely to be promoted within a year than is a minimum-wage worker putting in fewer than 10 hours per week.

Similarly, better-educated employees are more productive and therefore more likely to receive raises. Workers with college degrees who start at the minimum wage are 10 percentage points more likely to earn a raise within a year than are those who have not graduated from high school.

The notion that workers are trapped earning $5.15 an hour for much of their working lives is mistaken and ignores the true value of minimum-wage jobs. That value is not the wages that the jobs pay in the present, but the role that they play in introducing low-skilled workers into the workforce and providing them with the skills they need to advance in the economy.

Fewer Job Opportunities

The true minimum wage is always zero. A business can always choose not to employ a worker. A higher minimum wage boosts wages only for workers who could earn that wage without it. When the cost of hiring workers rises, however, businesses hire fewer workers. Some workers get a raise while others lose their jobs.

Most research on the minimum wage confirms this effect. A November 2006 paper examining this research found that two-thirds of recent studies of the minimum wage showed that it reduces employment, and all but one of the most reliable studies reached this conclusion.

Although individual studies give different estimates, the typical results from research suggest that a 10 percent increase in the minimum wage will reduce employment among heavily affected groups of workers by roughly 2 percent. One study of the effect of minimum wages on low-income workers found that each 10 percent increase would cost 1.2 percent to 1.7 percent of low-income workers their jobs. Another study found that in the long term, a 10 percent increase in the minimum wage reduces teenage employment by 2.7 percent. These estimates suggest that the proposed 40 percent hike in the minimum wage will cost at least 8 percent of intended beneficiaries their jobs.

More evidence of the job-destroying effect of the minimum wage comes from studies that examine state minimum-wage hikes. One recent study analyzed the effects of increases in the state minimum wage in Oregon and Washington. These states' economies are similar, and they increased their minimum wages at different times.

The researchers compared low-wage employment in Washington and in Oregon when Washington's minimum wage increased and when Oregon's increased. They found that the minimum wage strongly reduced employment in restaurants, where many workers earn the state minimum wage, but that it did not cost jobs in hotels, probably because most hotels in these states paid their employees more than the minimum wage both before and after the hikes. When the minimum wage rose, however, workers in industries that paid the minimum wage lost their jobs.

It is true that some studies have found that the minimum wage does not reduce employment, but most of these studies failed to measure the long-term effects of the minimum wage on employment. Instead, they looked at employment rates shortly before and shortly after the minimum wage increased and then concluded that the increase had little effect on employment.

Looking only at short-term job losses, however, does not reflect how businesses operate. For example, an alternative to hiring several unskilled workers is to hire just one skilled worker to perform the same task. Businesses begin to make this substitution when the minimum wage—and thus the cost of hiring unskilled workers—rises. Because businesses need time to update their production processes to use skilled labor, job losses do not immediately follow a minimum-wage hike. Thus, higher minimum wages destroy a significant number of jobs, not immediately but within a year or two of being passed. Studies showing that minimum-wage hikes do not cost jobs three months after they take effect prove only that their full effects take time to be felt in the economy.

A Disadvantage to Unskilled Workers

Another serious drawback of minimum-wage hikes is that they discourage companies from hiring the very workers who need the jobs the most. Minimum-wage workers earn low wages because they have fewer skills than other workers. They earn less because they are less productive. They are the workers who most need entry-level jobs so that they can gain experience and develop their skills.

When the government raises the minimum wage, it forces companies to pay their least-skilled workers the same amount as they pay their more-skilled workers. Given the choice between hiring an unskilled worker or a more productive worker for the same hourly rate, companies choose the worker who is more productive. Thus, higher minimum wages make it particularly difficult for unskilled workers to find work. Much research confirms this effect.

Long-Term Consequences

Because higher minimum wages deny unskilled workers entry-level jobs, they have long-term consequences. A worker who does not gain experience today could be at a competitive disadvantage for years.

Further, research shows that raising the minimum wage causes some teenagers to drop out of school to take jobs, replacing less-skilled workers in those positions. The less-skilled workers lose experience, and the teenagers forgo the benefits of education—a loss that will harm them throughout their careers.

This has led economists to examine the long-term consequences of raising the minimum wage. One study examined the earnings and employment of adult workers who were teenagers when their states raised the minimum wage above the federal level. For over a decade after passage, higher minimum wages lowered these workers' earnings and their likelihood of holding a job. The reduced number of entry-level jobs and increased high-school dropout rates mean that higher minimum wages hurt workers long after they become law.

Raising the minimum wage is well intentioned but counterproductive and will not help disadvantaged and unskilled workers get ahead. Many of the benefits flow to teenagers and young adults, not to the most needy, few of whom hold steady, full-time jobs. The minimum wage also does little to benefit disadvantaged workers because most of what they would gain from higher wages would then be lost because of reductions in government benefits.

The minimum wage exacts a steep price for its ineffectiveness. It destroys jobs and discourages employers from hiring the least-skilled and least-experienced workers who most need the work. This impact puts these workers at a disadvantage for years after an increase. Good intentions are not enough. Congress should look out for disadvantaged workers by refusing to increase the minimum wage.

> *"Since 1996, welfare caseloads have plummeted by 70 percent—8.8 million people off the rolls, which today are down to 3.8 million."*

Welfare Reform Has Reduced Poverty

Steven Malanga

In the following viewpoint, Steven Malanga writes that welfare reform—which prioritizes job placement—motivates and prepares the unemployed to return to the workforce, thereby reducing joblessness and poverty. The "work-first" philosophy and its requirements to search for employment or participate in job training brought dramatic declines to welfare rolls across the country, asserts Malanga. And over the last decade, welfare reform has been reauthorized—further restricting requirements for benefits—but he speculates that the administration of President Barack Obama will undo this progress. The author is a contributing editor to City Journal *and a senior fellow at the Manhattan Institute for Policy Research, a conservative think tank.*

As you read, consider the following questions:

1. What does Debra Autry claim about the impact of welfare reform on her life?

2. What changes resulted from the Budget Reconciliation bill (Deficit Reduction Act of 2005), as described by Malanga?

3. What does the work-first philosophy maintain as the biggest obstacle to employment, in Malanga's view?

In social-services jargon, Debra Autry had "multiple barriers to work" when the state of Ohio told her that she had to start earning her welfare benefits. Autry had been out of work and on public assistance for more than two decades, and she lacked many of the skills necessary for a modern economy. She was a single mother, too, like most welfare recipients, with three kids at home. Autry was skeptical about working in the private sector, so the state placed her in a publicly subsidized program that had her cleaning government offices in exchange for her benefits. Disliking the work, Autry landed a cashier's job at a local Revco drugstore, arranging her hours around her children's school day. After the CVS chain bought out Revco, she enrolled in the company's program to learn how to become a pharmacy technician and eventually began working in that position, which typically pays between $25 and $30 per hour. Autry's hard work inspired her children. Her daughter just earned a degree as a physical therapist, while one son is in college and another is working full-time. "I was on welfare because there were no jobs that interested me," she recalls. "But once I had to go back to work, I realized there's a future if you want to better yourself. It was the best decision I ever made."

Autry's story is the kind that reformers dreamed about back in 1996, when President Bill Clinton signed the federal Personal Responsibility and Work Opportunity Reconciliation

Act, often referred to as the welfare reform act. That legislation, drawing on earlier innovations in Wisconsin and New York City, time-limited aid and required some recipients to work, seeking to end the culture of long-term dependency that no-strings-attached public assistance had helped foster. Autry's success story turned out to be one of many. Since 1996, welfare caseloads have plummeted by 70 percent—8.8 million people off the rolls, which today are down to 3.8 million.

In fact, during the first few years of welfare reform, the rolls fell so quickly that many state welfare agencies, which administer welfare for the federal government, stopped feeling pressure to move their remaining welfare clients back into the workforce. But since 2005, states have further reformed their welfare programs to comply with a controversial reauthorization of the 1996 legislation that required states to move even more people to work. This next, crucial phase of welfare reform could put an end to traditional cash welfare assistance in all but the most extreme cases.

That is, unless Democratic policy makers get in the way. Ominously, Democratic foes of welfare reform have gathered power both in Congress and in President [Barack] Obama's cabinet.

Enormous Flexibility

The 1996 welfare legislation gave states enormous flexibility in fulfilling its requirements, and many interpreted the law liberally. Some counted as "work" the hours that recipients spent in treatment for alcohol or drug addiction or in traveling to and from job-training sessions. Others let recipients satisfy work obligations by "helping a friend or relative with household tasks or errands," according to a 2005 Government Accountability Office study. Certain states allowed home exercise, "motivational reading," and antismoking classes to qualify recipients for aid, reasoning that such practices could at least lead to work.

Despite such laxity, 4 million welfare recipients left the rolls during the first two years after President Clinton signed the reform into law. Since many states previously had required virtually nothing of welfare clients, simply compelling them to meet with caseworkers to discuss work options was enough to propel many out the door to look for jobs. "Everyone underestimated the ability of single mothers to go back to work," says Grant Collins, former deputy director of the Office of Family Assistance in the Department of Health and Human Services (HHS).

The number of leavers was so big, in fact, that it all but eliminated many states' federal requirements to keep moving people off welfare. The legislation required states' work-participation rates—that is, the percentage of people on welfare who were working or searching for work—to be at least 50 percent. But states were allowed to diminish that fraction by whatever percentage their welfare rolls had shrunk since 1995. By 2002, welfare rolls nationwide had fallen so steeply that 33 states could meet their obligations with work-participation rates of less than 10 percent.

Reenergizing Welfare Reform

That undesirable situation led to a three-year battle to reauthorize and reenergize welfare reform. The result was the 2005 Budget Reconciliation [bill; officially the Deficit Reduction Act of 2005], which changed the year from which states could calculate case reductions from 1995 to 2005, thereby ending the generous credit that most states enjoyed from their huge initial drop in welfare cases. Between 40 and 50 percent of states' adult welfare recipients now had to go back to work, search for a job, or otherwise prepare to work. The federal government also tightened the definition of what counts in fulfilling the work requirement: no longer would spending time in psychological counseling or in traveling to job training do the trick. And the feds urged states to enroll more welfare recipients with physical or mental disabilities in job-training and job-placement programs. "Individuals who happen to have disabilities should be afforded the same opportunities to engage in work—to find work-related training, work experience, and employment—as those who do not have a disability," the [George W.] Bush administration's Department of Health and Human Services wrote in its new regulations.

Advocates and some pols [politicians] charged that many of those remaining on welfare were too troubled for states to hit the demanding new work-participation targets. [National] Urban League president Marc Morial complained that the bill would "subject families to harsher work requirements with inadequate funding" for social services to help them adjust. He scored the bill in particular for limiting how long someone could remain on welfare while pursuing a college degree. "We don't have many families left. Those remaining have multiple issues," objected the head of Welfare Advocates, a Maryland-based coalition of social-services agencies and churches. A 2002 Urban Institute study that found that 44 percent of welfare recipients faced two or more "barriers to work" became a frequent citation.

HHS had basically discounted such complaints in writing its new welfare regulations, in part because the critics were defining "barrier to work" too loosely. The Urban Institute study, for instance, considered the lack of a high school diploma, being out of the workforce for three or more years, and lack of English proficiency as obstacles to work, while other groups argued that being a single parent was a major barrier. A common demand was that welfare programs first provide day-care services for single parents or treatment for addicts before requiring any work. "I was at a White House conference in the mid-1990s in which someone observed that we couldn't require single mothers on welfare to go back to work until we had day care for all of them," recalls Peter Cove, cofounder of America Works, an employment service for welfare recipients.

"I stood up and said that if we tried to solve every problem before asking people to work, we'd never get any recipient back in the workforce."

The "Work-First" Philosophy

The 2005 bill wholly embraced this "work-first" philosophy. Work-first originally emerged as a welfare reform model in the 1980s, adopted by Wisconsin governor Tommy Thompson; in the mid-nineties, Mayor Rudy Giuliani enthusiastically signed on in New York City. At its core, work-first maintains that the biggest obstacle that many welfare clients face to employment is their own lack of understanding of the fundamentals of any workplace—showing up for work regularly and on time, for instance. The best way to help such people isn't to put them in elaborate job-training programs, this approach holds, but simply to get them working—even in entry-level positions—under the careful supervision of a caseworker, who makes sure that they get up in the morning and out the door. Caseworkers will even help out with recipients' child-care emergencies or get alcoholic clients to continue in treatment—but all with the aim of keeping them on the job. "Many of the best therapeutic programs for people with problems like alcoholism don't think it's a good idea for people to stop working and go home and sit on a couch all day after counseling," says Tom Steinhauser, head of Virginia's welfare division. "Why should welfare programs treat people any different?"

A work-first approach has helped sustain deep reductions in New York City's welfare population, long after rolls stopped dropping in some states. By the time Rudy Giuliani left office in 2001, the city's welfare numbers had fallen from 1.1 million to 475,000, and they're down another 25 percent, to 339,000, under Mayor Michael Bloomberg, who has continued the reforms. Many of those who wind up on welfare today remain "work-ready," argues Robert Doar, commissioner of Gotham's

Human Resources Administration (HRA), which is why the city has been able to place some 70,000 to 80,000 of them a year in jobs.

The "work-ready" population is evident at the crowded Manhattan offices of America Works, where I went to observe cofounder Lee Bowes address a new group enrolled in the organization's counseling and employment program. Every seat is taken, and even the windowsills are occupied. When one attendee asks why the classroom is so crowded, Bowes bluntly responds: It's because lots of people are looking for jobs. Asked by Bowes how she wound up on welfare, a single mother explains that her apartment building burned and that she and her children found themselves temporarily homeless. She then lost her job and went on public assistance; she says that she's ready, though, to get back to work. Is this the first agency that she has visited since going on welfare, Bowes wonders? The woman's answer elicits nods from the group: "I went somewhere where they treated me like I was in kindergarten. They asked me if I was ready to go back to work. I said yes—can you help me find a job? Then I heard that this place does that. So I'm here now."

On the Road to Independence

Most of these welfare recipients will wind up in entry-level jobs. The average starting wage for someone coming off welfare in New York is just slightly above $9 an hour, according to the HRA. But with other assistance, like the federal and state earned income-tax credits, food stamps, and Medicaid, a recipient's actual annual income can rise well above $20,000—not enough for an extravagant lifestyle in New York, of course, but enough to allow her to get back on her feet and start down the road to independence. This aid menu is typical across the country, even if assistance levels vary. With the decline in welfare rolls, states now spend more on noncash assistance programs, like food stamps, than on welfare itself.

Many employers have tapped this labor pool because it has been hard for them to fill entry-level positions. New York City–sponsored job fairs for welfare recipients attract dozens of companies. America Works says that it has a reliable list of employers ready to hire welfare recipients for entry-level jobs. Even in an economic downturn, like the current one or the national recession that began in mid-2001, employers keep seeking entry-level workers because of the high turnover rate for these jobs. Welfare rolls didn't rise in New York City during the last recession, it's worth noting. . . .

Stricter Standards

Under the revised welfare rules, however, states can no longer ignore such employers and their jobs, and more states are re-shaping their programs along work-first lines. Over the last two years [2007 to 2009], for instance, 17 states have created more stringent contracts for local private agencies working with welfare recipients, requiring them to meet job-placement targets or risk penalties. Arizona has told its contractors that if the federal government penalizes the state for failing to meet work goals, the contractors must share in the punishment. Private groups must even prove when bidding for Arizona contracts that they have sufficient financial reserves to pay any fines. But the state will also give bonuses to agencies that perform job placement well.

Several states have imposed stricter standards even on their own public agencies. In California, new legislation lets the state pass on to county welfare offices any financial penalties that it might incur for failing to meet the new federal regulations. County administrators also must file plans explaining how they intend to meet their new requirements, and county work-participation rates now get shared throughout the system, so everyone can see how each county is performing. Pennsylvania, which had a dismal 7 percent work-participation rate for its approximately 40,000 adult welfare recipients in 2005, not only has started grading each county program but publishes the entire list online.

States are also requiring welfare applicants to begin job searches or undergo employment counseling much more quickly than in the past. Eleven states have altered application procedures to include some kind of employment assessment for people when they first request welfare. New applicants in Delaware, for instance, must spend two weeks working with an employment and training counselor before receiving benefits. Missouri no longer considers a welfare application complete unless the applicant has met with an employment counselor and worked out a job-search plan.

In many states, welfare recipients once could keep getting benefits even when they refused to comply with work or vocational requirements, an enormous impediment to reform. Since the 2005 legislation, however, ten states that previously only partially reduced a welfare recipient's check for failing to participate in such programs have now moved to "full sanctions," that is, cutting off benefits completely. Other states, while not going as far, have implemented harsher penalties or are at least considering doing so. . . .

Agencies are also taking a harder look at programs that try to get those who claim to have physical or mental barriers to work on the path toward employment. Sometimes this means encouraging them to begin part-time work or to undergo counseling to see what kind of training and work they might qualify for. "States are doing things that sound really simple, like having their own doctors assess those who claim they can't work," says Jason Turner, who designed Wisconsin's welfare-to-work programs and is now a Milwaukee-based consultant. "But you would be surprised how many states were merely accepting notes from a welfare recipient's doctor, excusing them from work." . . .

Fighting the Battle Again

The new law gave states two years to comply, starting from mid-2006, when the feds issued the specific regulations outlining states' obligations. Many states, including Pennsylvania, Maryland, and Virginia, say that they've raised their work-participation rates substantially since then and are close to complying, though the feds have yet to issue a report on the states' progress.

Yet no one knows how Barack Obama's White House— which brings with it a whole new set of administrators at the Department of Health and Human Services under the new secretary, former Senate majority leader Tom Daschle[1]—will carry out the law. As a senator, Daschle opposed the original 1996 welfare reform and then stalled its reauthorization from 2002 through his 2004 electoral defeat. Obama, meanwhile, turned down several opportunities during the presidential campaign to say whether he would have signed the welfare reform act if he had been president in 1996; he preferred not to look back, he said, but forward. During the campaign, he did run ads crediting the 1997 Illinois law that he helped write— which brought the state's welfare system in line with federal changes—with Illinois's decline in welfare caseloads.

Congress's most powerful Democrats have also opposed welfare reform. Speaker of the House Nancy Pelosi voted against both the 1996 legislation (calling it "punitive and unrealistic") and the 2005 bill. Harry Reid, the current Senate majority leader, has used language strikingly similar to that of social-services advocates to criticize welfare reform. On its tenth anniversary, he declared that "many welfare recipients face significant barriers to employment" and that states need "flexibility" in aiding them.

At the very least, such statements suggest that a Reid-and-Pelosi-controlled Congress could unwind some key elements of the 2005 law, such as the restrictions on counting certain

1.*Daschle withdrew his nomination on February 3, 2009.*

kinds of job training or substance-abuse counseling as work, when welfare reform again comes up for reauthorization in 2011. Such moves would almost certainly inflate work-participation rates artificially and blunt some of the effectiveness of the 2005 reforms. Whether Congress would attempt to go further, digging into the original 1996 legislation and curtailing some of its mandates, is hard to predict at this stage. But the fact that Obama and his new HHS secretary have hardly been enthusiastic in their support for welfare reform suggests that we may have to fight the battle for it all over again.

> *"As millions are being thrown out of their homes and losing their jobs, state governments are reducing the meager assistance available to the poor and unemployed."*

Welfare Reform Has Increased Poverty

Fred Goldstein

Fred Goldstein is a contributing editor to Workers World, *the newspaper for the Workers World Party, and author of* Low-Wage Capitalism: Colossus with Feet of Clay. *In the following viewpoint, Goldstein argues that welfare reform has plunged millions into poverty. Starting with President Bill Clinton's administration in the 1990s, policy changes have driven households—largely single mothers and minorities—off welfare to divert the cash to the ruling class and create an exploitable low-wage workforce, he alleges. Even as unemployment rose during the recent recession, Goldstein contends, welfare caseloads reached a historic low in 2009, hurting the jobless and poor.*

As you read, consider the following questions:

1. According to Goldstein, what was the status of welfare in the states with high unemployment in early 2009?

2. What happened to workers under the Temporary Assistance for Needy Families program, as told by Goldstein?

3. What is the author's opinion of the new law that set a fixed amount for the national welfare bill?

As millions are being thrown out of their homes and losing their jobs, state governments are reducing the meager assistance available to the poor and unemployed.

Some 2.6 million jobs were lost in 2008. The announcement of 500,000 to 600,000 more layoffs in January [2009] is expected soon and hundreds of thousands of job cuts are already slated for February.

Yet the number of people getting cash assistance during this crisis remained "at or near the lowest in 40 years." An article in the Feb. 2 *New York Times* reported the grim figures.

Eighteen states actually cut their welfare rolls in the midst of the crisis. Michigan, one of two states with official unemployment of more than 9 percent, cut its welfare rolls by 13 percent. Of the 12 states where unemployment grew most rapidly, eight of them either cut the rolls or kept them the same.

Of the 10 states with the highest child poverty rates, eight kept caseloads level or further reduced the rolls. Five states had double-digit reductions in the welfare rolls, including Texas, which ended assistance to 15 percent of recipients.

These cuts, primarily aimed at women, come at a time when joblessness among women without a high school degree and aged 20 to 24 rose to 23.9 percent—from 17.9 percent a year ago. Celia Hagert of the Center for Public Policy [Priorities] in Austin, Texas, told the *Times*, "We're really just pushing families off the program."

Rhode Island closed the cases of 2,200 children because their families had been on the rolls longer than the 60-month lifetime limit.

Bill Clinton Destroyed Welfare, Pushing Millions into Poverty

The program under which welfare benefits are dispensed is called Temporary Assistance for Needy Families (TANF). This draconian program was put in place in 1996 under the [President Bill] Clinton administration. It replaced a 60-year-old program initiated during the New Deal entitled Aid to Families with Dependent Children (AFDC).

Bill Clinton came to office pledging to "end welfare as we know it." That was shorthand for "We shall destroy welfare." And that is what Clinton did, in a bloc with the Republican-controlled Congress under the leadership of right-wing reactionary Newt Gingrich. After signing the law, Clinton gloated that "The era of big government is over."

Of course, Clinton did not mean the "big government" of the Pentagon, the FBI, the CIA, etc. What he did was carry out a long-sought-after goal of the ruling class: letting them get their hands on the cash that had been given to single mothers with children who were left under capitalism to flounder on their own in poverty. They further wanted to drive millions of impoverished women off the rolls in order to create a vast, low-wage, highly exploitable addition to the workforce.

Under AFDC, women with children who met conditions of low or no income, as well as individual men with low or no income who were unemployable, were entitled to apply for assistance. The cash assistance was minimal and the process of applying for it was cumbersome and degrading. Submitting to harassing, invasive monthly inspections to retain your benefits was even more degrading. Since the benefit was primarily for single mothers, women had to conceal any relationship with a male just to keep the pittance doled out by the capitalist state.

Nevertheless, AFDC was vital to the existence of millions of women and their children. Because of generations of racist discrimination, they were disproportionately African American and Latina, but millions of poor white families also benefited. It was a basic support at the level of survival. And it was guaranteed by law to anyone who qualified.

Under Clinton the entitlement came to a cruel end. TANF gave block grants in fixed amounts to the states to pretty much do with as they pleased. The states were required to move millions of poor women off the rolls in infamous "welfare to work" programs. Many reactionary governors relished the prospect of driving into the workforce these poor women, who often wound up forced to take low-paying, menial jobs either in the public or private sector.

Workers had to put in a full week at these low-paying jobs to earn diminished welfare benefits and could only get them for five years total during their lifetime. Women who tried to go to school to get a skill were often forced to choose between benefits and school if their education forced them to reduce their work hours.

The bill was so draconian that Assistant Secretary of Health and Human Services Peter Edelman resigned in protest and wrote a long indictment in the March 1997 issue of the *Atlantic* entitled "The Worst Thing Bill Clinton Has Done."

At that time this author wrote an open letter to Edelman in the March 27, 1997, issue of *Workers World* newspaper entitled "Let's Overturn the Welfare Law."

Our letter said in part: "We are inclined to agree with the title of the article . . . [although Clinton] has done many terrible things. These include the crime bill with its funding for prisons, police and capital punishment; the anti-terrorism bill that increased the FBI's repressive power and did away with the right of habeas corpus; extending the criminal blockade of

Cuba by signing the Helms-Burton Act; continuing the murderous sanctions against Iraq and many other reactionary measures."

The letter cited how Edelman showed that "a total of 11 million families—10 percent of all American families—would lose income under the bill. This included more than 8 million families with children, many of the working families affected by food-stamp cuts, which would average about $1,300 per family."

"You show," continued the letter, "that almost 800,000 immigrants will lose Supplemental Security Income [SSI] benefits and food stamps to the tune of $24 billion over six years. And that 100,000–200,000 disabled children, mostly those with multiple disabilities, will lose SSI."

Edelman said at the time, "This is hardly a welfare bill . . . these are just cuts" for poor and working families.

The open letter concluded with a call to point the finger at the Pentagon, the bankers and the capitalists and to call forth a movement to overturn the law.

The Other Shoe Has Dropped

Most importantly, the new law set a fixed amount for the total national welfare bill, regardless of how many people needed assistance. Not only was this totally vicious, highly racist and unjust at the time, but it inevitably would lead to disaster for all workers. The minute there was an economic crisis and the workers ran out of unemployment benefits, the masses of unemployed would be plunged into dire poverty and suffering.

Now the country is in the midst of an enormous and growing economic crisis that is engulfing wider and wider sections of the workers. But because of the Clinton destruction of welfare, with the switch from AFDC to TANF, caseloads have fallen every year since 1994. The present level of 4.1 mil-

Not a Human Capital Approach

Since TANF's [Temporary Assistance for Needy Families'] creation federal policy has incorporated a "work first" approach emphasizing immediate employment in any available job, rather than a human capital approach encouraging the education and training that lead to steady employment in living wage jobs. States incur a financial penalty if they do not place a specified minimum percentage of recipients in federally countable activities for a specified minimum number of hours. High school attendance generally counts as full participation only if the parent is under age 20, and college attendance as full participation only if the program of study qualifies as "vocational education" and then only for 12 months. In 2008, fewer than 2% of adult recipients were counted as participating based on high school/GED [General Educational Development] attendance, and only about 4% were counted as participating based on attendance in vocational education.

"Welfare Reform at Age 15:
A Vanishing Safety Net for Women and Children,"
Legal Momentum, April 2011. www.legalmomentum.org.

lion has not been seen since 1964. The fact is that cash benefits paid out under TANF as of October 2008 were only 30 percent of the benefits that had been paid out under AFDC.

The Clinton group has largely moved into the present administration, including Hillary Rodham Clinton and [former White House chief of staff] Rahm Emanuel, among others. This is the group that helped Clinton and Gingrich wield the ax that fell upon the workers and the oppressed and that is intensifying suffering now.

The only road to reverse this devastating onslaught against the workers and the oppressed is to mobilize a massive fight-back campaign that demands not only minimal benefits, but the full guarantee of a job at living wages with benefits or a livable income. This should be the true entitlement of the multinational working class.

"*[The American Recovery and Reinvestment Act] will soften the blow on poor Americans while also preventing millions of people from falling into poverty.*"

The American Recovery and Reinvestment Act Will Reduce Poverty

James Kvaal and Ben Furnas

James Kvaal is the deputy undersecretary of education and former senior fellow at the Center for American Progress, where Ben Furnas was a research associate. In the following viewpoint, Kvaal and Furnas contend that the American Recovery and Reinvestment Act, enacted in 2009, will prevent millions of people from falling into poverty during the recession. Tax cuts for the poorest households and tax credits for almost all taxpayers will provide relief to many middle- and low-income families, the authors state. Furthermore, add Kvaal and Furnas, these benefits have a greater impact on the economy, as low-income families are more likely to spend additional income on necessities rather than save.

As you read, consider the following questions:

1. What signs of hard economic times do the authors provide?

2. How will the act enhance unemployment benefits, as stated by the authors?

3. What figures do the authors cite to support their claim that tax cuts and benefits to low-income families help the economy more than those to high-income families?

The American economy is in a recession that is 14 months old [in February 2009], and the downturn appears to be growing deeper and more severe. Approximately 1.8 million Americans lost their jobs in the past three months alone—nearly 20,000 a day. It's increasingly looking like "the worst recession since World War II" may be a best-case scenario.

The economic downturn means hard times for millions of Americans. If unemployment rates reach double-digits, as some economists fear, nearly 7 million people will lose their jobs, more than 7 million will lose their health coverage, and more than 12 million will fall into poverty.

The economic recovery legislation before Congress would cushion the blow for the most vulnerable families by cutting taxes and strengthening the safety net, while boosting the economy and creating jobs to make the middle class stronger and larger. Helping struggling families is not only the right thing to do in hard times; it is also one of the most cost-effective ways to fight the recession. Aid for low-income families generates five times more economic activity than aid for high-income families, according to some estimates, because these families are more likely to spend the money immediately on necessities rather than saving it.

Rising Unemployment Leaves Millions of American Families Struggling

The six years of economic expansion before the recession began in December 2007 never reached millions of Americans. Thirty-seven million people were living in poverty in 2007—4 million more than when the economic expansion began in 2001. Real median household income grew by only 0.26 percent a year throughout the years of economic expansion, which kept income below 2000 levels. And nearly 7 million people lost their health insurance during that period.

Now the economy has turned sour. It has shrunk by 3.6 million jobs since the recession began 13 months ago. There are 11.6 million people out of work—the third-most since 1949. Leading indicators such as announced layoffs, inventories, and demand for temporary workers give no sign that job losses are beginning to slow. And the International Monetary Fund warns that the advanced economies may already be in a "depression."

Signs of hard times are clear across the country. The number of homeless families is growing at double-digit rates in many cities. Demand for free and reduced price lunches in California has surged by 12 percent since last year—12 times the normal rise—and other school districts are seeing similar increases. In Miami, Florida, 1,000 job applicants stood in line for 35 firefighter positions, and in Hartford, Connecticut, 850 people applied for fewer than 50 jobs at a hotel and water park.

The economy could get far worse without quick action. The Congressional Budget Office projects that the unemployment rate could reach 9 percent in 2010. Some private sector forecasters are more pessimistic. Mark Zandi of Moody's Economy.com expects the unemployment rate to exceed 11 percent in 2010 and the economy to lose nearly 7 million jobs.

Rising unemployment rates mean that millions of families will struggle to make ends meet. Increases in poverty are sure to follow. . . . Unemployment and poverty rates have historically risen together.

More than 12 million Americans are at risk. The number of people living in poverty will rise by 12.4 million by 2010—including 3.8 million children—if the unemployment rate reaches 11 percent, according to our analysis based on a methodology developed by the Center on Budget and Policy Priorities. And more than 7 million people will fall into deep poverty, living below half of the poverty line.

Dramatic increases in poverty are consistent with past recessions. The number of people living in poverty grew by 9 million between 1979 to 1983, and it grew by 8 million between 1989 and 1993.

The weak job market will also raise the number of people without health insurance. A percentage-point increase in unemployment could raise the number of uninsured by 1.1 million. If unemployment rates rise according to Moody's projections—increasing from 4.6 percent in 2007 to 11.1 percent in 2010—more than 7 million people will likely lose their health insurance.

The Recovery Package Would Help Vulnerable and Middle-Class Families

The American Recovery and Reinvestment Act would provide immediate assistance to help vulnerable families and prevent millions of middle-class Americans from falling into poverty. It would also stimulate the economy and create jobs, helping many additional families avoid poverty.

Tax cuts

The bill would cut taxes for low-income working families. It would expand the earned income tax credit—America's largest antipoverty program. The credit matches wages earned by low-income families, encouraging them to work and offsetting payroll taxes. Expanding the credit for families with three or more children would make nearly 1 million families eligible for the credit and give tax relief to a total of nearly 7 million.

It would also expand the child tax credit for the poorest working families, many of whom are ineligible for the credit today because their incomes are too low. By eliminating the income threshold, the House legislation would benefit 17 million children. The less generous Senate bill, which only lowers the eligibility threshold from $8,500 to $8,100, would provide significantly less help to fewer children.

Together, these two tax cuts could make a large difference in the lives of the poorest families. The Recovery and Reinvestment Act would lift 2.5 million Americans out of poverty, according to the Center on Budget and Policy Priorities' analysis of the House version of the bill. No analysis is available for the Senate bill.

Another important tax credit is the Making Work Pay credit, which is a $500-per-worker tax cut for nearly all taxpayers. The credit would make a meaningful difference for both middle-class and low-income families.

Unemployment insurance and help for households

The recovery legislation would also help straggling Americans by expanding unemployment insurance so that the long-term unemployed can continue to receive benefits through the end of 2009. It also offers states financial incentives to modernize their unemployment eligibility rules, which disproportionately disqualify jobless low-wage and part-time workers. These changes would benefit 18 million unemployed workers, including 3 million who would otherwise be denied any claims at all.

Both the House and Senate bills also include help for other households. Both bills increase food stamp payments. The Senate bill includes one-time payments to Social Security recipients, poor people on Supplemental Security Income, and veterans receiving disability and pensions. And the House bill includes similar payments to poor elderly and disabled people.

Other important provisions for low-income families include child care assistance for working parents, Head Start programs to prepare low-income children for school, and Pell grants and tax breaks to make college more affordable. Assistance to state governments would prevent tax increases and cuts to crucial services. And new resources would help low-income families insulate their homes and pay their heating bills.

House vs. Senate legislation

The resolution of the differences between the House and Senate proposals will affect the final bill's overall effectiveness. The two packages are similar in size, but the Senate version spends more on tax cuts that will do less for both working families and the economy as a whole.

The House legislation does more to expand the child tax credit for poor working families. Current law denies this credit to millions of children who need it most. The Senate legislation wipes out the majority of these gains, providing less help to fewer children.

The Senate bill also provides $40 billion less for states facing massive budget deficits, half the amount provided by the House bill. States are facing $350 billion in deficits over the next two and a half years. The resulting huge spending cuts and tax increase will impose hardships on working families and undermine the economic recovery.

The Senate bill is less generous in other areas as well. It does less to stabilize neighborhoods devastated by foreclosures, retrofit public housing, cover unemployed workers with health insurance, and enroll young children in Head Start. It meanwhile gives larger tax breaks to money-losing companies, which the Congressional Budget Office believes will have little or no impact on the economy.

The Recovery Package Would Boost the Economy

Helping working families will not only keep millions of families out of poverty; it is also one of the most cost-effective ways to boost the economy and create jobs. As a result, it would strengthen and expand the middle class.

Tax cuts and transfer payments to families only generate economic activity if they are spent rather than saved. Low-income families are most likely to spend the additional income, and policies aimed at low-income households therefore tend to do more for the economy. One dollar for low-income people—including unemployment insurance, nutrition assistance, and refundable tax credits—adds between $0.80 and $2.20 to the economy, according to the Congressional Budget Office. A dollar of tax cuts for high-income households adds only between $0.10 and $0.50 cents.

The recovery legislation makes investments that will create jobs now and promote economic opportunity in the years to come. Both the House and Senate bills include a historic investment in renewable energy and energy efficiency that will immediately begin to create "green jobs" and continue promoting sustainable, affordable energy for decades. Both include nearly $50 billion for roads, public transit, and public housing. And both would allow a new wave of investment in our schools and colleges that will strengthen education and promote future growth.

Our economy is in a perilous state. Millions of middle-class families are likely to fall into poverty if Congress does not take swift action. The American Recovery and Reinvestment Act will make the middle class larger and more secure by strengthening the safety net and sparking economic activity to create jobs and raise wages. As a result, it will soften the blow on poor Americans while also preventing millions of people from falling into poverty.

Periodical and Internet Sources Bibliography

The following articles have been selected to supplement the diverse views presented in this chapter.

Joyce Appleby   "Living Wages Are Key to Poverty Eradication," *Los Angeles Times*, June 14, 2010. www.latimes.com.

Michelle Chen   "Urban Communities Seek Lift Through Living Wage," *In These Times*, December 22, 2009. www.inthesetimes.com.

Peter Edelman   "The Next War on Poverty," *Democracy*, no. 15, Winter 2010. www.democracyjournal.org.

Elaine Kamarck   "No Time to Go Wobbly on Welfare Reform," *Ten Miles Square* (blog), *Washington Monthly*, September 19, 2011. www.washingtonmonthly.com.

Kelly O'Connell   "To Revive US Economy, Remove Minimum Wage in American Poverty Centers," Canada Free Press, September 18, 2011. www.canadafreepress.com.

Lizzy Ratner   "The Failure of Welfare Reform Is 'Exhibit A' That the Right's Punish-the-Poor Philosophy Doesn't Work," AlterNet, August 29, 2011. www.alternet.org.

Robert Rector   "Losing the War," *National Review Online*, March 16, 2010. www.nationalreview.com.

Peter Schiff   "Minimum Wage, Maximum Stupidity," LewRockwell.com, July 13, 2009. www.lewrockwell.com.

Cal Thomas   "Time to Rethink 'War on Poverty,'" *USA
and Bob Beckel   Today*, September 22, 2010. www.usatoday.com.

OPPOSING
VIEWPOINTS®
SERIES

CHAPTER 4

How Should Global Poverty Be Addressed?

Chapter Preface

In 2000 all member states of the United Nations (UN) and numerous international organizations adopted the Millennium Development Goals (MDGs) to fight global poverty and its effects. Composed of eight goals to achieve by 2015, the first MDG is to eliminate extreme poverty and hunger. It includes three targets: to halve the proportion of people, between 1990 and 2015, who earn and live on less than one dollar a day; to create productive and fair employment for all, including women and youths; and to halve the proportion of people who go hungry.

The UN released a progress report in 2011, stating that the MDG of halving poverty is within reach. "Despite significant setbacks after the 2008–2009 economic downturn, exacerbated by the food and energy crisis, the world is still on track to reach the poverty-reduction target. By 2015, it is now expected that the global poverty rate will fall below 15 per cent, well under the 23 per cent target,"[1] the UN declares. According to the report, China will have poverty rates decrease to below 5 percent by the goal date, and India will have poverty rates fall to 22 percent, compared to 51 percent in 1990. As for sub-Saharan Africa, the projections "are slightly more upbeat than previously estimated. Based on recent economic growth performance and forecasted trends, the extreme poverty rate in the region is expected to fall below 36 per cent," the UN claims.

Nonetheless, these figures do not sway critics of the MDGs and their impacts on levels of poverty and third world economic development. "For example, what progress has been made in poverty reduction is largely thanks to pre-existing growth patterns in China and India, rather than policy efforts flowing from the MDGs per se,"[2] argues the Center for Economic and Social Rights (CESR). "The statistics on extreme poverty—based on 2005 data—do not capture the full impact of the global economic crisis, estimated by the World Bank to have plunged an additional 64 million people into extreme poverty since 2007," CESR maintains. In the following chapter, the authors examine how nations, businesses, and individuals respond to global poverty.

Notes

1. United Nations, *The Millennium Development Goals Report 2011*, 2011. www.un.org.
2. Center for Economic and Social Rights, "MDG Failures Prove Need for a New Rights-Based Development Agenda," July 14, 2011. www.cesr.org.

| "We not only need more money to fight poverty, we need more coherence in our policy approach."

Foreign Assistance Can Reduce Global Poverty

J. Brian Atwood

In the following viewpoint, J. Brian Atwood declares that international development cooperation, or foreign assistance, can alleviate global poverty through partnerships with poor countries to spur development and reform. International development cooperation can tap into a nation's potential for wealth creation, he continues, which makes the available resources (land, labor, and capital) more productive. This can be achieved by bolstering social services, attacking economic and political corruption, and supporting democratic institutions, states the author. Atwood is chair of the Development Assistance Committee of the Organisation for Economic Co-operation and Development (OECD) and former administrator of the US Agency for International Development (USAID).

As you read, consider the following questions:

1. In Atwood's opinion, what attitude does the word "aid" spread about foreign assistance?

2. What analogy does Atwood use to explain his strategy in fighting global poverty?

3. What are the seven sources of wealth, as described by the author?

I am very pleased that you have chosen to focus on poverty. This is one of the globe's greatest challenges—right up there with climate change, terrorism, and nuclear proliferation. In fact, alleviating the conditions of poverty is part of the solution to those other great challenges of our day.

You have asked me, "Is Aid the Answer?" Let me begin my answer by quibbling over your use of words. The word "aid" as in "foreign aid" is passé. It is inappropriate language, even harmful to the task of alleviating poverty.

The terminology in use today is "international development cooperation," and words do matter. This connotes a real partnership with the developing world. And, yes, if that partnership exists, development cooperation is very much a part of the answer—not the whole answer, but a part of the answer.

The other reason I dislike the word "aid" is that it reflects a widespread attitude in the West that assistance devoted to alleviating poverty is a "gift" from rich nations to poor ones. The gift mentality stands in the way of cooperation; it implies that a nation's behavior is somehow being rewarded; and it creates an aura of conditionality that sends the message: *Made in the West*.

The other side of the "gift" coin is the problem of dependency. Development assistance is transitional. It can be a catalyst to reform and development, but it can never be a substitute for a nation's commitment to its own development. Even the poorest nations should be investing a high portion of their own revenues on development. They should never become dependent on official development assistance (ODA).

Five Points of Foreign Assistance

So, where do I stand on the spectrum of opinion on development assistance personified by economists Jeff Sachs and Bill Easterly? Sachs wants to ramp up the volume of assistance and Easterly sees failure in traditional approaches and worries that more aid will inflate currencies and create dependency. Of course, each of these distinguished economists has a more complex position, but the titles of their books and articles lend themselves to simplistic interpretations. One, Sachs, likes to portray himself as the optimist. Easterly is the pessimist.

You can portray me as the realist—and I have the scars to prove it! Let me make five points:

1. An argument has been made that foreign assistance has been a failure over the past 50 or so years. Easterly has made that case in a typical economist's fashion—he has measured economic growth rates and the accumulation of wealth against the investments that have been made. What he leaves out is the progress made in agriculture, infant mortality rates, availability of potable water, the increased accessibility of family planning, and other health and nutrition interventions. Yes, there has been some waste. That is inevitable when you are dealing with very difficult challenges. But the question should be "What would the world look like today had we not made the investments?" [Development expert] Carol Lancaster argues that a 70% success rate is what a venture capitalist aims for. That is the success rate of foreign assistance. Not bad.

2. Second, much of the waste Easterly cites occurred because foreign aid—that is what it was called then—was

both an experiment in the early days and a political tool during the Cold War. The first experiments with assistance involved concepts that were top-down, concepts like the "rising expectations" and "hierarchy of needs." Our theorists paid little attention to the poor. The East-West conflict created a political competition when developing nations were pawns in a game that only incidentally included poverty alleviation. Authoritarian leaders in poor countries became quite adept at playing both sides while excluding their own people from having a meaningful role in development. There was no international consensus on the goals for development. Today there is. The U.N. Millennium Development Goals represent that consensus. Yet they will never be reached by 2015 if we continue on today's path. As a UNDP [United Nations Development Programme] report stated, the world is "heading for a heavily sign-posted human development disaster." There should be no question that an increase in the volume of ODA is needed if these goals are to be reached as Sachs has suggested. However, that is only a part of the solution.

3. Cooperation on the ground is essential . . . participatory development works as Easterly suggests, but the people must be empowered to speak and act for themselves. Global goals can only be reached through local action. Development is not a top-down exercise, either globally or nationally.

4. The West and the developing nations too often are like ships passing in the night when defining the global agenda. For example, we look at the issue of security differently. We in the West see security as terrorism and weapons of mass destruction. Developing nations believe that the predominant security threat is poverty. They see the Millennium Development Goals as vital. We often

seem to be paying only lip service to them, but have even been prepared in the past few years to abandon them to acquire leverage in negotiations to reform the U.N.

5. Finally, if we are going to give new impetus to the effort to alleviate poverty, we need to avoid sweeping denunciations of our past efforts. Easterly's book *The White Man's Burden* should be used as a critical analysis of what has gone before. But it is more likely to be used to justify doing nothing more.

Sachs' book *The End of Poverty* is an effort to rally the international community and I commend him for that. However, advocacy should be grounded in today's realities. One cannot simply gloss over these difficult issues without attempting to see the other side.

My preference is for books like [economics professor] Paul Collier's *The Bottom Billion* and [chief economist of the US Agency for International Development] Steve Radelet's *Challenging Foreign Aid*. These books contain policy prescriptions that are based on empirical data and solid analysis. They are grounded in practice.

Development Is Not a Mystery

But you came here to hear my views, not hear me cite the views of others. I believe that poverty is an enormous, singular threat that the international community ignores at its own peril.

I also believe that we are falling far behind in our efforts to deal with this problem despite recent major increases in the volume of assistance that is available. The international community needs to get its act together and to organize around some basic principles. Let me share a few ideas:

What Will Happen If We Are Wrong?

International aid is necessary in order to end extreme poverty. Though some may argue that the impoverished should "pull themselves up by the bootstraps," this is not possible when the population is simply fighting to survive. China and India have often been pointed to as evidence of how countries can succeed without (some even say in spite of) international aid. This is a fair claim; however, the implications of this conclusion are disheartening. If international aid is not offered, and we leave the third world to find its own way to prosperity, what will happen if we are wrong?

If international aid is not offered to these countries and they are unable to grow by themselves, their natural resources will continue to deplete, their population will continue to grow, and the situation will only become worse. On the other hand, giving money to stop the spread of disease, money to improve educational opportunities, money to grow the stock of capital, money to introduce technology is a plausible response to the poverty and suffering of the third world.

Kristine Koutout,
"Is It Plausible for International Aid to End Extreme Poverty
in Our Generation?," Clemson University-Management,
May 23, 2008. http://cujo.clemson.edu.

1. Let's not make development such a mystery. Development is about making "land, labor, and capital more productive." The Development Assistance Committee of OECD [Organisation for Economic Co-operation and Development] describes ODA as the transfer abroad of public resources on concessional terms . . . , a significant objective of which is to bring about an improvement in

economic, political, or social conditions in developing countries. So that is the "what." The "how" is more complicated. That is part two.

2. What we need is information and analysis for each developing country. This is a major challenge and not enough ODA resources [are] available to perform that task. I call it a "diagnostic," to borrow a medical term.

Let me use an analogy that may be more understandable to non-experts. What if you were a general—let's say the Chairman of the U.S. Joint Chiefs—and you were confronted with a new threat, weapons of mass destruction in the hands of a dictator in a poor country. You would want to know everything about the country: its terrain, its ethnic groups, its trade patterns, its regional allies, even its cultural habits.

Then you would want appropriate weapons systems, soldiers with the right kind of training, language experts, and, most importantly, good intelligence.

Then, after you got deeply involved against an asymmetric threat—an indigenous terrorist group—you would appeal for more troops. Maybe you would call it a "surge."

Then you would tell the public that you seek "victory." And anyone who doesn't buy this argument gets to be called a defeatist. That is my Iraq editorial!

Well, if poverty is as serious a threat to global stability as we believe it is, why shouldn't we have the best information possible about the countries and regions where it resides? Why shouldn't we have the best tools to fight it? Why shouldn't we have the "surge capacity" to defeat it? And what is wrong with aspiring to a victory over time?

The Seven Sources of Wealth

Let's start with our diagnostic. My friend, Michael Fairbanks, developed an excellent tool for framing assessments of a nation's potential for wealth creation. He calls it the Seven

Sources of Wealth:

1. Natural endowments (location, climate, forests, etc.)

2. Financial resources (savings, reserves)

3. Humanly made capital (buildings, bridges, roads, power plants)

4. Institutional capital (rule of law, parliaments, courts, government departments, etc.)

5. Knowledge resources (think tanks, universities, labs, patents, etc.)

6. Human capital (skills, educated workforce)

7. Cultural capital (attitudes, values)

All nations share these attributes to some degree. The first three are more easily measurable. In general, there are three things foreign assistance can help with as part of a "surge" against poverty in cooperation with solid partners in poor countries:

1. Human capacity: health care, family planning and education. Often poor countries can't afford these basic social services.

2. Attack the informal economy and corruption creating transparent and efficient microeconomic systems: banking systems that make loans to micro and small businesses; tax systems that are highly progressive and fair; commercial laws that eliminate arbitrary government behavior and encourage production and growth; customs and legal systems that facilitate exports and imports; legal protections for private property; create a rule of law culture.

3. Democratic institutions that enable citizen participation, fair representation even for minorities, and efficient, responsive government.

These things cannot be done easily and cannot be done by donors alone. But they, along with the Millennium Development Goals, provide the agenda for international development cooperation.

Unfortunately, unlike the general who can draw from a $600 billion defense budget for his surge, donors have much less to draw upon—about $75 billion is the total for the Western donors. And people are needed—development professionals. The U.S., for example, has fewer diplomats and development officers than our military has in its bands and choirs.

A More Coherent Approach

We not only need more money to fight poverty, we need more coherence in our policy approach.

The West spends about $1 billion a year on agricultural development in poor countries while spending $1 billion a day on various subsidies for its own agriculture sector. We need to open our markets.

Our finance ministries push stability and fight inflation through the IMF [International Monetary Fund], but too little attention is given to providing the flexibility for development. Are we more interested in protecting Western investment than in helping nations create jobs and growth?

We are at the tipping point. You have seen the statistics. This world cannot survive with half its people living in poverty. This condition of poverty is directly threatening the prosperity and relative stability the world has achieved in the past fifty years. We cannot put our heads in the sand or just pass U.N. resolutions which we promptly ignore. It is time for a major global surge to alleviate poverty.

I am looking for young recruits. Who wants to enlist?

> "But unfortunately, despite all these good intentions, if the conditions for aid's proper use do not prevail, that aid is more likely to harm than help the world's poorest nations."

Foreign Assistance Cannot Reduce Global Poverty

Jagdish Bhagwati

Jagdish Bhagwati is a senior fellow in international economics at the Council on Foreign Relations and University Professor of economics and law at Columbia University. In the following viewpoint, Bhagwati insists that foreign assistance cannot alleviate global poverty. He maintains that aid has been wasted and spent by corrupt regimes, and discussions of aid and development exclude policy makers and experts from developing countries. Instead, Bhagwati recommends that liberal policy reforms should be enforced to reduce global poverty and aid should be channeled to support the adoption of sound policies and countries that can use it properly.

As you read, consider the following questions:

1. What is Bhagwati's position on the principles of foreign aid?

2. How did foreign aid fuel corruption during the Cold War, as described by the author?

3. How did China and India reduce poverty without foreign assistance, in the author's view?

If you live in the affluent West, no public policy issue is more likely to produce conflicts in your conscience than foreign aid. The humane impulse, fueled by unceasing televised images of famine and pestilence in the developing world, is to favor giving more aid. But a contrasting narrative has the opposite effect: Emperor Jean-Bédel Bokassa of the Central African Republic used Western aid to buy a gold-plated bed, and Zaire's dictator, Mobutu Sese Seko, spent it on personal jaunts on the Concorde. Such scandals inevitably lead many to conclude that most aid is wasted or, worse still, that it alone is responsible for corruption.

These debates have largely been the province of Western intellectuals and economists, with Africans in the developing world being passive objects in the exercise—just as the 1980s debate over the United States' Japan fixation, and the consequent Japan bashing, occurred among Americans while the Japanese themselves stood by silently. Yet now the African silence has been broken by Dambisa Moyo, a young Zambian-born economist with impeccable credentials. Educated at Harvard and Oxford and employed by Goldman Sachs and the World Bank, Moyo has written an impassioned attack on aid that has won praise from leaders as diverse as former UN secretary-general Kofi Annan and Rwandan president Paul Kagame.

Moyo's sense of outrage derives partly from her distress over how rock stars, such as Bono [of the group U2], have dominated the public discussion of aid and development in recent years, to the exclusion of Africans with experience and expertise. "Scarcely does one see Africa's (elected) officials or those African policy makers charged with a country's development portfolio offer an opinion on what should be done," she writes, "or what might actually work to save the continent from its regression. . . . One disastrous consequence of this has been that honest, critical and serious dialogue and debate on the merits and demerits of aid have atrophied." She also distances herself from academic proponents of aid, virtually disowning her former Harvard professor Jeffrey Sachs, whose technocratic advocacy of aid and moralistic denunciations of aid skeptics cut no ice with her. Instead, she dedicates her book to a prominent and prescient early critic of aid, the development economist Peter Bauer.

Moyo's analysis begins with the frustrating fact that in economic terms, Africa has actually regressed, rather than progressed, since shedding colonial rule several decades ago. She notes that the special factors customarily cited to account for this tragic situation—geography, history, social cleavages, and civil wars—are not as compelling as they appear. Indeed, there are many places where these constraints have been overcome. Moyo is less convincing, however, when she tries to argue that aid itself has been the crucial factor holding Africa back, and she verges on deliberate provocation when she proposes terminating all aid within five years—a proposal that is both impractical (given existing long-term commitments) and unhelpful (since an abrupt withdrawal of aid would leave chaos in its wake).

Moyo's indictment of aid, however, is serious business, going beyond Africa to draw on cross-sectional studies and anecdotes from across the globe. Before buying her indictment, however, it is necessary to explore why the hopes of donors have so often been dashed.

The Charity Trap

Foreign aid rests on two principles: that it should be given as a moral duty and that it should yield beneficial results. Duty can be seen as an obligation independent of its consequences, but in practice, few are likely to continue giving if their charity has little positive effect. Beginning in the years after World War II, those who wanted the rich nations to give development aid to poorer ones had to address the challenges of building domestic support for greater aid flows and ensuring that the aid would be put to good use. But their unceasing efforts to produce higher flows of aid have led aid advocates to propose the use of tactics that have ironically undermined aid's efficacy, virtually guaranteeing the kind of failures that understandably trigger Moyo's outrage.

At the outset, aid was principally driven by a common sense of humanity that cut across national boundaries—what might be called cosmopolitan altruism. Aid proponents in the 1940s and 1950s, such as Gunnar Myrdal and Paul Rosenstein-Rodan, were liberals who felt that the principle of progressive taxation—redistribution within nations—ought to be extended across international borders. This led to proposals such as those to set an aid target of one percent of each donor nation's GNP [gross national product] playing off the Christian principle of tithing (giving ten percent of one's income to the church) or the Muslim duty of zakat (which mandates donating 2.5 percent of one's earnings to the needy).

How was the one percent figure arrived at? According to Sir Arthur Lewis, the first Nobel laureate in economics for development economics, the British Labour Party leader Hugh Gaitskell had asked him in the early 1950s what figure they should adopt as the United Kingdom's annual aid obligation and Lewis had settled on one percent of GNP as a target because he had a student working on French colonies in Africa, where French expenditures seemed to add up to one percent of GNP. Such a target, of course, implied a proportional, rather than a progressive, obligation, but it had a nice ring to it.

The problem was that the one percent target remained aspirational rather than practical. Outside of Scandinavia, there was never much popular support for giving away so much money to foreigners, however deserving they might be. So aid proponents started looking for other arguments to bolster their case, and they hit on enlightened self-interest. If one could convince Western legislatures and voters that aid would benefit them as well, the reasoning went, the purse strings might be loosened.

In 1956, Rosenstein-Rodan told me that then Senator John F. Kennedy, who bought into the altruism argument, had told him that there was no way it could fly in the U.S. Congress. A case stressing national interest and the containment of communism was needed. And so the argument was invented that unless the United States gave aid, the Soviet Union would provide it and, as a result, the Third World might tilt toward Moscow. In fact, the Soviets had already funded the construction of Egypt's Aswan Dam, a project the United States had turned down. The only catch was that if the Cold War became Washington's rationale for giving aid, it was inevitable that much of it would end up in the hands of unsavory regimes that pledged to be anticommunist—regimes with a taste for gold-plated beds, Concordes, fat Swiss bank accounts, and torture. By linking aid payments to the Cold War, proponents of aid shot themselves in the foot. More aid was given, but it rarely reached the people it was intended to help.

From Altruism to Self-Interest

When the Cold War began to lose its salience, the search began for other arguments to support aid. The World Bank appointed two successive blue-ribbon panels to deliberate on ways of expanding aid flows, the Pearson Commission [on In-

Corruption and Waste at Every Stage

Last but not least, when the money reaches a designated recipient—a bridge builder, a teacher, or a farmer—that recipient must spend it wisely. The bridge builder must build the bridge; the teacher must show up at school; the farmer must use his fertilizer. None of these can be taken for granted. Indeed, the lesson of development economics of the last decade is that there is tremendous corruption, waste, and resource misallocation at every stage. Bridges are not built (or collapse soon after if built); teachers stay at home; and farmers retain old production techniques.

Andrei Shleifer,
"Peter Bauer and the Failure of Foreign Aid,"
Cato Journal, vol. 29, no. 3, Fall 2009.

ternational Development], in 1968, and the Brandt Commission, in 1977. The group led by former West German chancellor Willy Brandt, although emphasizing that there was a moral duty to give, fell back nonetheless on an enlightened self-interest argument based on a Keynesian [based on the theories of economist John Maynard Keynes] assertion that made no sense at all: that raising global demand for goods and services through aid to the poor countries would reduce unemployment in the rich countries—an argument seemingly oblivious to the fact that spending that money in the rich countries would reduce unemployment even more.

Other feeble arguments related to immigration. It was assumed that if aid were given wisely and used effectively, it would reduce illegal immigration by decreasing the wage differentials between the sending and the receiving countries. But the primary constraint on illegal immigration today is the inability of many aspiring immigrants to pay the smugglers who shepherd them across the border. If those seeking to reach El Norte or Europe earned higher salaries, they would have an easier time paying "coyotes," and more of them would attempt illegal entry.

Lewis, who was a member of the Pearson Commission, therefore despaired of both the altruistic and the enlightened self-interest arguments. I recall him remarking in 1970, half in jest, that development economists should simply hand over the job of raising aid flows to Madison Avenue. Little did he know that this is exactly what would happen 20 years later with the advent of the "Make Poverty History" campaign, supported by Live Aid concerts and the sort of celebrity overkill that many Africans despise. Of course, this has meant the revival of the altruism argument. Aid targets have therefore returned to the forefront of the debate, even though they are rarely met: in 2008, there was a shortfall of $35 billion per year on aid pledged by the G-8 countries [a forum for the governments of eight major economies] at the Gleneagles summit in 2005, and the shortfall for aid to Africa was $20 billion.

One of the chief reasons for the gap is not just miserliness but a lack of conviction that aid does much good. Aid proponents today try to overcome this doubt by linking aid-flow obligations to worldwide targets for the provision of primary education and health care and other laudable objectives enshrined in the 2000 UN Millennium Development Goals (which are uncannily reminiscent of the Brandt Commission's proposals). But the question Moyo and other thoughtful critics properly insist on raising is whether aid is an appropriate policy instrument for achieving these targets. . . .

Paved with Good Intentions

Similar problems involving the mismatch between intentions and realities are present in today's battles over aid. Now, as before, the real question is not who favors helping the poor or spurring development—since despite the slurs of aid proponents, all serious parties to the debate share these goals—but rather how this can be done.

Many activists today think that development economists in the past neglected poverty in their quest for growth. But what they miss is that the latter was seen as the most effective weapon against the former. Poverty rates in the developing countries did indeed rise during the postwar decades, but this was because growth was sporadic and uncommon. And that was because the policy framework developing countries embraced was excessively dirigiste [directed by a central authority], with knee-jerk government intervention across the economy and fears of excessive openness to trade and foreign direct investment. After countries such as China and India changed course and adopted liberal (or, if you prefer, "neoliberal") reforms in the last decades of the century, their growth rates soared and half a billion people managed to move above the poverty line—without question, the greatest and quickest progress in fighting poverty in history.

Neither China nor India, Moyo points out, owed their progress to aid inflows at all. True, India had used aid well, but for decades its growth was inhibited by bad policies, and it was only when aid had become negligible and its economic policies improved in the early 1990s that its economy boomed. The same goes for China.

If history is any guide, therefore, the chief weapon in the "war on poverty" should be not aid but liberal policy reforms. Aid may assist poor nations if it is effectively tied to the adoption of sound development policies and carefully channeled to countries that are prepared to use it properly (as President George W. Bush's Millennium Challenge program recently sought to do). Political reform is important, too, as has been recognized by the enlightened African leaders who have put their energies into the New Partnership for Africa's Development (NEPAD), which aims to check the continent's worst political abuses.

But unfortunately, despite all these good intentions, if the conditions for aid's proper use do not prevail, that aid is more likely to harm than help the world's poorest nations. This has been true in the past, it is true now, and it will continue to be true in the future—especially if some activists get their wishes and major new flows of aid reach the developing world simply because it makes Western donors feel good.

Moyo is right to raise her voice, and she should be heard if African nations and other poor countries are to move in the right direction. In part, that depends on whether the international development agenda is set by Hollywood actresses and globetrotting troubadours or by policy makers and academics with half a century of hard-earned experience and scholarship. In the end, however, it will be the citizens and policy makers of the developing world who will seize the reins and make the choices that shape their destiny and, hopefully, soon achieve the development progress that so many have sought for so long.

"Because so few people give significant amounts, the need for more to be given is great, and the more each of us gives, the more lives we can save."

Philanthropy Is a Necessary Response to Global Poverty

Peter Singer

Peter Singer is an Australian philosopher and bioethicist. In the following viewpoint, excerpted from his book The Life You Can Save: Acting Now to End World Poverty, *he asserts that philanthropy is needed to counter global poverty and save lives. Despite perceptions that America is a generous donor nation, Singer points out that it lags behind many countries in how much it gives in national income and private donations. Furthermore, he insists that practical, immediate aid is necessary to help the poor and stop the crisis from worsening. Singer states that even modest contributions can prevent millions of children from dying every year from poverty.*

As you read, consider the following questions:

1. How did the United States compare to other nations in donating national incomes in 2006, as told by Singer?

Peter Singer, *The Life You Can Save: Acting Now to End World Poverty.* New York: Random House, 2009, pp. 33, 35–40. Copyright © 2009 by Random House, Inc., and Palgrave Macmillan. All rights reserved. Reproduced by permission.

2. How does Singer respond to the argument that giving food and money to the poor creates dependency?

3. In what ways would poverty be impacted if everyone gave modest contributions, in Singer's view?

A merica is a generous nation. As Americans, we are already giving more than our share of foreign aid through our taxes. Isn't that sufficient?

Asked whether the United States gives more, less, or about the same amount of aid, as a percentage of its income, as other wealthy countries, only one in twenty Americans gave the correct answer. When my students suggest that America is generous in this regard, I show them figures from the website of the OECD [Organisation for Economic Co-operation and Development] on the amounts given by all the organization's donor members. They are astonished to find that the United States has, for many years, been at or near the bottom of the list of industrialized countries in terms of the proportion of national income given as foreign aid. In 2006, the United States fell behind Portugal and Italy, leaving Greece as the only industrialized country to give a smaller percentage of its national income in foreign aid. The average nation's effort in that year came to 46 cents of every $100 of gross national income, while the United States gave only 18 cents of every $100 it earned.

Asked what share of America's national income the United States gives in foreign aid, 42 percent of respondents believed that the nation gives more than four times as much as it actually gave, while 8 percent of Americans thought that the United States gives more than 100 times the actual amount!

A majority of people in these surveys also said that America gives too much aid—but when they were asked how much America should give, the median answers ranged from 5 percent to 10 percent of government spending. In other words, people wanted foreign aid "cut" to an amount five to ten times greater than the United States actually gives!

Some contend that these figures for official aid are misleading because America gives much more than other countries in private aid. But although the United States gives more private aid than most rich nations, even its private giving trails that of Australia, Canada, Ireland, and Switzerland as a percentage of national income, and is on a par with giving by people in Belgium and New Zealand. Adding U.S. nongovernmental aid, of 7 cents per $100 earned, to U.S. government aid leaves America's total aid contribution at no more than 25 cents of every $100 earned, still near the bottom of the international aid league.

Philanthropy vs. Political Change

Philanthropic responses undermine real political change.

If those on the right fear that I am encouraging the state to seize their money and give it to the world's poor, some on the left worry that encouraging the rich to donate to aid organizations enables them to salve their consciences while they continue to benefit from a global economic system that makes them rich and keeps billions poor. Philanthropy, philosopher Paul Gomberg believes, promotes "political quietism," deflecting attention from the institutional causes of poverty—essentially, in his view, capitalism—and from the need to find radical alternatives to these institutions.

Although I believe we ought to give a larger portion of our income to organizations combating poverty, I am open-minded about the best way to combat poverty. Some aid agencies, Oxfam [International] for example, are engaged in emergency relief, development aid, *and* advocacy work for a fairer global economic order. If, after investigating the causes of global poverty and considering what approach is most likely to reduce it, you really believe that a more revolutionary change is needed, then it would make sense to put your time, energy, and money into organizations promoting that revolution in the global economic system. But this is a practical question, and if there is little chance of achieving the kind of revolution you are seeking, then you need to look around for a strategy with better prospects of actually helping some poor people.

Giving and Dependency

Giving people money or food breeds dependency.

I agree that we should not be giving money or food directly to the poor, except in emergencies like a drought, earthquake, or flood, where food may need to be brought in to stop people from starving in the short term. In less dire situations, providing food can make people dependent. If the food is shipped in from a developed nation, for example the United States, it can destroy local markets and reduce incentives for local farmers to produce a surplus to sell. We need to make it possible for people to earn their own money, or to produce their own food and meet their other needs in a sustainable manner and by their own work. Giving them money or food won't achieve that. Finding a form of aid that will really help people is crucial, and not a simple task, but as we'll see, it can be done.

Giving Now, Not Later

Cash is the seed corn of capitalism. Giving it away will reduce future growth.

Gaetano Cipriano contacted me after reading one of my articles because he thought that as an entrepreneurial capitalist, he could offer a helpful perspective. The grandson of immigrants to America, he owns and runs EI Associates, an engineering and construction firm based in Cedar Knolls, New Jersey, that has assets of around $80 million. "Cash is the seed corn of capitalism" is his phrase. Gaetano told me that he deploys his capital to the best of his ability to promote profits and enduring growth, and that giving more of it away would

be "cutting my own throat." But he does not spend extravagantly. "I do not live in a splendid house," he told me. "I have no second home. I drive a 2001 Ford Explorer with 73,000 miles. I belong to a nice squash club, and have four suits and two pairs of black shoes. When I take vacations they are short and local. I do not own a boat or a plane." While he does give to charity, he does it "at a level which is prudent and balanced with sustainable growth." If he were to give much more money away, it would have to come out of sums that he now reinvests in his business. That, in turn, would reduce his future earnings and perhaps the number of people he is able to employ, or how well he can pay them. It would also leave him with less to give if, later in life, he decides that he wants to give more.

For similar reasons, we can agree that it's a good thing [investor] Warren Buffett did not give away the first million dollars he earned. Had he done so, he would not have had the investment capital he needed to develop his business, and would never have been able to give away the $31 billion that he has now pledged to give. If you are as skilled as Buffett in investing your money, I urge you to keep it until late in life, too, and then give away most of it, as he has done. But people with less-spectacular investment abilities might do better to give it away sooner.

Claude Rosenberg, who died in 2008, was founder and chairman of RCM Capital Management, an institutional money management firm, so he knew something about investing, but he also knew a lot about philanthropy. He founded a group called New Tithing and wrote *Wealthy and Wise: How You and America Can Get the Most Out of Your Giving*. He argued that giving now is often a better value than investing your money and giving later, because the longer social problems are left unchecked, the worse they get. In other words, just as capital grows when invested, so the costs of fixing social problems are likely to grow. And, in Rosenberg's view, the rate at which the cost of fixing social problems grows is "exponentially greater" than the rate of return on capital. In support of this belief, Rosenberg pointed to the cascading impact of poverty and other social problems, not just on one person but on future generations and society at large. The claim is a broad one, difficult to prove or disprove; but, if it is true for poverty in the United States, then it is even more likely to hold for poverty in developing countries, in part because it is easier to get a high percentage return when starting from a low base. Of course, that assumes that there are things we can do in developing countries that will be effective in reducing poverty.

Modest Contributions from Everyone

What if you took every penny you ever had and gave it to the poor of Africa . . . ? What we would have is no economy, no ability to generate new wealth or help anybody.

This objection comes from Colin McGinn, a professor of philosophy at the University of Miami. It isn't clear whether McGinn's "you" is you, the individual reader, or the group an American Southerner might refer to as "y'all." If you [insert your name], took every penny you ever had and gave it to the poor of Africa, our national economy would not notice. Even if every reader of this book did that, the economy would barely hiccup (unless the book's sales exceed my wildest dreams). If *everyone* in America did it, the national economy would be ruined. But, at the moment, there is no cause for worry about the last possibility: There is no sign of it happening, and I am not advocating it.

Because so few people give significant amounts, the need for more to be given is great, and the more each one of us gives, the more lives we can save. If everyone gave significantly more than they now give, however, we would be in a totally different situation. The huge gulf between rich and poor means that if everyone were giving, there would be no need for them to take every penny they ever had and give it all to Africa. . . . Quite a modest contribution from everyone who has enough to live comfortably, eat out occasionally, and buy bottled water, would suffice to achieve the goal of lifting most of the world's extremely poor people above the poverty line of $1.25 per day. If that modest contribution were given, we would no longer be in a situation in which 10 million children were dying from poverty every year. So whether a small number of people give a lot, or a large number of people give a little, ending large-scale extreme poverty wouldn't cripple our national economy. It leaves plenty of scope for entrepreneurial activity and individual wealth. In the long run, the global economy would be enhanced, rather than diminished, by bringing into it the 1.4 billion people now outside it, creating new markets and new opportunities for trade and investment.

Caring for Family and the Poor

> People do have special relationships with their families,
> their communities, and their countries. This is the standard
> equipment of humanity, and most people, in all of human
> history, have seen nothing wrong with it.

—Alan Ryan, philosopher and warden of New College, Oxford

It is true that most of us care more about our family and
friends than we do about strangers. That's natural, and there
is nothing wrong with it. But how far should preference for
family and friends go? Brendan, a Glennview High student,
thought that instead of going to aid for the poor, money "can
be better spent helping your family and friends who need the
money as well." If family and friends really *need* the money, in
anything remotely like the way those living in extreme poverty
need it, it would be going too much against the grain of human nature to object to giving to them before giving to strangers. Fortunately, most middle-class people in rich nations
don't have to make this choice. They can take care of their
families in an entirely sufficient way on much less than they
are now spending, and thus have money left over that can be
used to help those in extreme poverty. Admittedly, saying just
where the balance should be struck is difficult.

> "The Idea of Philanthropy is much more attractive than the actual thing, and unfortunately it is much more widespread."

Philanthropy Is a Flawed Response to Global Poverty

Vinny Singh

In the following viewpoint, Vinny Singh suggests that philanthropy has become an ideal instead of an act, encouraging dangerous complacency toward global poverty. He argues that merely "caring" is perceived as good in itself and satisfies the consciences of those who passively confront the poor and their dire conditions. However, Singh continues, caring is not enough, and many people stop short of engaging in philanthropic action. When the viewpoint was originally published, the author was a student at Rice University and contributor to its student magazine, the Rice Standard.

As you read, consider the following questions:

1. What did Singh's group do after visiting a Nicaraguan slum?

Vinny Singh, "The Idea of Philanthropy: The New 'It' Thing," *The Rice Standard*, March 16, 2011. Copyright © 2011 by Manasvini Singh. All rights reserved. Reproduced by permission.

2. How is the public's perception of charity formed, in Singh's view?

3. Why does Singh not place blame on people for placing their own lives over others?

Managua, Nicaragua: It is a sign of the unawareness of extreme poverty when an incident bringing two countries to international court is unknown to the majority of both countries. The story of how Nemagon, a pesticide imported from America, united thousands of banana farmers in Nicaragua in a battle over one of the largest health catastrophes in the country has been fighting a losing battle against the tide of time. The incident is one of many Aesop's fable-like incidents that warn against the evils of corporationism and capitalism—but pain, especially of others, is easily forgotten. Our group, which is normally based in Costa Rica, went to the capital of Managua for a week where we were witness to the Nemagon Protest, a huge slum settlement squatted on government grounds. They have been protesting for the past six years against the injustice of using a pesticide in Nicaragua long after it was banned in America. Hundreds of affected former plantation workers carried on the fight to convince the Nicaraguan government to ask for compensation from Shell Chemical Corporation, the company that trademarked this soil fumigant that has killed thousands of farmers since 1857. In the unbearable heat infested with flies and mosquitoes, these unheard-of martyrs live in makeshift houses of cardboard. Most of them show signs of extreme age and now have children carrying on their fight for them—but there are also people who show signs of extreme sickness. Mutilated knees, twisted backs, untreated cancers, blindness, disfigured skins—all are evidence of those for whom capitalism failed.

Forgotten for Good

I am from India. Not in the sense that I am Indian in ethnicity or even nationality—which I am—but in a whole different way. I was born in India, and I grew up in India and while India itself is ravaged enough by extreme poverty, it took a long time for even my family to finally be able to afford and indulge in basic luxuries that I am living and reveling in now. I know that my parents have known poverty, and even more so my grandparents before them—and it is in that knowledge itself that I know the value of money, and of comfortable living, and never taking anything for granted. I have seen poverty in a way that nobody can see just by visiting a squatters settlement for forty minutes.

Thus, it was not initially the sheer poverty that captivated me. What interested me more was the variety of responses that accompanied our tour of the ramshackle little abode of over 500 poor Nicaraguans. There were tears on many faces, a general hush over the group as we moved from one cardboard separation to the other, some colorful language in response to the dire poverty, and angry expressions so recognizable on faces of activists. As we left the precariously held-up establishment, I heard voices of outrage, fear, disgust, disbelief. I heard voices talking about writing to the senators of their states. Some talked of contacting Greenpeace. Others were discussing sending e-mails to their universities to ask for aid.

So it is solely in that spirit that I interjected into the heated conversation that was going on after we had just witnessed the Nemagon Protest and asked them what we could do to help the protestors right at that very moment. While I knew before I asked the question what the answer would be, it was still unsettling to face it. Absolute silence. I tried again.

"Could we perhaps all donate some money?"

"Perhaps."

In ten minutes, we were boarding the bus. In another ten minutes we had left the area. Before we knew it, we were talking about what we were going to eat for lunch. The Nemagon protesters were forgotten for good.

Looking out of the window at the utility poles and trees rushing past us, I wondered what I had personally felt looking at those people. Sadness? Anger? Disbelief? Yes, a little bit of all them. But I think, most of all, I felt a sense of déjà vu. When I see such things, it is always followed by helplessness, and then immediately by cynicism. Reflecting back at how I felt meandering past the Nemagon settlement, I am surprised that I didn't feel more emotion. I always thought that having come from a country like India, I would feel more connected to the sufferings of the world.

Is it a sign of how much my heart has been hardened over the years that I was able to mount the bus and leave the quagmire of wretchedness that I had just seen? Or have I developed a defense mechanism against the misery I have seen so far in the world, just so I wouldn't break down every time I was brought right up close and personal to it? Or (how hard this is to put down in writing!) have I just become completely apathetic, with these words being my final gasps for air in the illusions of comfort and warmth that I am drowning in right now? The only source of comfort right now is that I still have enough of a conscience to be able to think about it, and write about it, and feel some stirrings deep within myself still. Is that enough for the rest of my life? Of course not. But at nineteen years of age, it gives me hope that my conscience is that seedling that will sprout into a lush green verdant canopy of empathy when I grow up—when I do have the option of staying back and not getting onto that bus and just driving away.

Talk Is Talk

But then, if almost everybody has a conscience, why is there still so much poverty in the world? Why has the image of the malnutritioned, dust-covered, naked "black baby" lost its ability to elicit shock? Why were we able to forget about Nemagon so easily? Then I realized that ultimately, talk is talk, and it is easier to feign concern than actually let the fact hit home that there are people all over the world who live like this. After all, we would then actually need to *do* something. In essence, people are lazy, and people do not like being shaken out of their little idea of a perfect world even though there is undeniable proof of how perfect is perhaps the last word to describe the world we live in. The reason people ignore the devastation that is being caused by global warming is the same reason people don't believe it when somebody tells them that their loved one is cheating on them. Nobody likes to be pushed outside their comfort zone, because the truth of what lies outside their little cocoons can be extremely uncomfortable.

Everybody *knows* about poverty, malnutrition, climate catastrophes and the other ills of the world. And in daily conversation it is a subject that causes a great many emotions and sympathy, but the basic emotion of empathy is lacking. Too much evil is happening in the world for anybody to ignore it completely. Apathy is socially unacceptable now. No longer can you say, "Who cares?" or "Well, that doesn't really affect me." Apathy is now just another synonym for ignorance. Apathy is lumped with just another of the many vices that have been morally blacklisted—like greed, lust and conceit before it. It has almost become "cool" to care. [Investor] Warren Buffett donated $31 billion to the Bill & Melinda Gates Foundation, and both Buffett and Gates have persuaded 34 American billionaires to pledge away half of their wealth to charity during their lifetimes. Mark Zuckerberg, the youngest billionaire and almost already a historic youth icon, has pledged half of his wealth to charity.

In a society constantly bombarded by a media more concerned with Hollywood than with Third World issues, it is not surprising that the common man's perception of charity is formed by Angelina Jolie's publicized role as the UN goodwill ambassador and her adoption of children from countries like

Cambodia, Ethiopia and Vietnam. We are socially coded to copy people we respect or admire most. In reaction to seeing some of the wealthiest, most famous or most talented people in the world care about global issues, we have immediately followed suit.

The Idea of Philanthropy

However, while we have moved away from complete apathy, we haven't quite made it to the other side just yet. The Idea of Philanthropy has become a mask for the actual thing. It is so much easier to express horror or shock at an earthquake that killed thousands of people rather than pack up your bags and head out to Haiti to help distribute food. It is so much easier to talk about donating money than actually doing it. I have been guilty of this, as have been so many other people. There *are* people who dedicate their lives to helping out people less fortunate than them—and it is solely these people who have ushered in this era of philanthropy.

The Idea of Philanthropy is much more attractive than the actual thing, and unfortunately it is much more widespread. What really worries me is that this state of mind is undoubtedly so much more dangerous than the state of apathy most people are used to. While apathy clearly delineates the segregation between the people who care and the people who don't, pretending to care just leads to more sociological complications. More people are encouraged to just talk about philanthropy, which solely serves a self-fulfilling motive. Consciences begin to feed on the satisfaction people get just by thinking they care, because both religion and society state that "caring" is good, and "not caring" is bad. But what no religious books or any community actually talk about is how just "caring" does not serve the actual final purpose of "helping." "Caring" is just an ego booster. People feel better about themselves if they are moved by genocide in Rwanda because they feel that it is a sure indicator of the fact that they still have a conscience, that they still have a soul. People who do not care about such things have obviously sold themselves to the devil—what kind of person feels nothing watching large-scale slaughter? But everybody forgets that philanthropy is not supposed to be a morale-raiser for the giver. It is only intended for the receiver. And so philanthropy ends up being a scale by which people measure their own "goodness", and thus becomes an idea, instead of an action.

While I do not deny that much of philanthropy feeds a person's sense of self-worth—indeed I'm sure that many people donate to charities to ensure their "place in heaven" or to raise their social standing—it is one thing to have an ego boost because you worked in Ghana for orphans, and a completely different thing to have an ego boost only because you were capable of having the wish to work in Ghana for orphans. It sounds confusing, but it is actually quite simple: "Caring" is not enough. It is the first step to philanthropy, maybe—but it is by no means the last. "Caring" enough to actually "do" something about whatever it is that made you care, is what real philanthropy is all about. People all over the world are stopping midway on their roads to philanthropy, and I am scared that if enough people stand on the line between apathy and empathy, nobody will be able to see past the crowd to their final destination.

Life goes on quickly, and [Charles] Darwin's rule of Survival of the Fittest is the major factor against philanthropy. I am sure people want to help, that they do indeed feel for the thousands of the people affected daily by the curses of the world, but people have their own lives to live and their own worries to deal with. In all honesty, one cannot really blame them for placing their own lives over some incident that is happening half a world away from them. Most of us do not have enough money to have the luxury to donate significantly or to start foundations. Animal behaviorologists have proven that true altruism doesn't really exist in the animal world, so I have to grudgingly accept the fact that we probably will never be able to truly care about another human being in the same way that we care about ourselves. The maxim, "Love thy neighbor as you do thyself," will never actually be truly realized. But then, I always did think that we're just a little more evolved than animals. Perhaps we may yet surprise ourselves.

| "Microfranchising has proved useful in bridging the last mile in the delivery of vital goods and services."

Microfranchising Can Be a Solution to Global Poverty

PRWeb

PRWeb is a company that distributes press releases online. In the following viewpoint, BRAC—the world's largest development organization—believes that microfranchising and microfinance will help end global poverty. BRAC develops easily replicated business strategies in poor communities that create a network of microentrepreneuers. Through this network, these poor communities can earn extra income and provide social good.

As you read, consider the following questions:

1. What approach does Sir Fazle Hasan Abed favor toward job creation?

2. According to the viewpoint, how many of the world's poorest families received a microloan in 2010?

3. Why did BRAC begin its experiments with microfranchising, according to the viewpoint?

B RAC, the world's largest development organization, lays out its "microfinance plus" approach to defeating global poverty at the Global Microcredit Summit 2011 in Valladolid, Spain, this week [in November 2011]. Presenting BRAC's strategy to over 2,000 delegates at the annual microfinance conference, Sir Fazle Hasan Abed, the founder and chairperson, advocates a market-oriented approach to job creation and poverty alleviation that puts poor borrowers on a path to prosperity by giving them a "business in a box."

It's an approach that development experts call "microfranchising." Working in poor communities, BRAC develops sustainable business models that can be easily replicated, creating networks of self-employed micro-entrepreneurs who earn extra income by delivering vital services that achieve a social good.

BRAC's Global Network

More than 137.5 million of the world's poorest families received a microloan in 2010, an all-time high, according to the Microcredit Summit Campaign. BRAC itself reaches over 8 million borrowers, a number rising steadily thanks in part to this year's launch of bKash Limited, a mobile financial service provider in Bangladesh and a subsidiary of BRAC Bank, the organization's bank targeting small businesses.

But development organizations should think beyond microfinance to make strides against poverty, BRAC's founder says. "Financial services alone are not sufficient to break the bonds of poverty," says Abed, who launched BRAC in Bangladesh in 1972. In a paper presented at the conference, Abed explains how BRAC has combined microfinance with agricultural services to improve rural livelihoods and food security in Bangladesh and around the world.

Now in 10 countries, BRAC has built a global network of 150,000 microfranchised entrepreneurs providing services in agriculture, poultry, livestock and health. Abed calls it a "holistic, sustainable, market-oriented approach" to poverty alleviation that uses microloans, training and branding, while offering borrowers low-cost access to inventory, efficient distribution systems and continuous support.

"BRAC provides the branding, inventory and training to the micro-entrepreneurs, who in turn provide training and product to BRAC microfinance clients and others in the villages where BRAC operates," writes Abed and co-authors Dr. Mahabub Hossain, Susan Davis, and Rod Dubitsky in the paper, "Using Microfinance Plus Agricultural Services to Improve Rural Livelihoods and Food Security," which will appear in the forthcoming volume *New Pathways Out of Poverty*. . . .

"The entreprencurs, in turn, earn income by selling the goods BRAC provides at a markup. For example, BRAC entreprencurs earn between $15 and $20 per month in the provision of poultry vaccination services. Farmers in turn get a valuable service and expect to benefit by enjoying a material drop in poultry mortality. Such a 'Business in a Box' not only provides a valuable service and income, it is a more sustainable model than other programs that provide vaccines free (which may not be available to all farmers and may not be reliably available)."

Microfranchising has proved useful in bridging the last mile in the delivery of vital goods and services, says Susan Davis, the president and CEO of BRAC USA and one of the paper's co-authors. "A poor person can find a bottle of Coca-Cola today anywhere in rural Africa—but not mosquito bed nets and condoms," says Davis. "Distribution is a real challenge that organizations never speak about, but it is one of the most critical hurdles in reaching the poor. Microfinance institutions can effectively bridge this gap. For instance, BRAC reaches more than 8 million women, every week—at their doorstep, in providing credit and financial services. Can you imagine the potential of a sustainable distribution model like this?"

BRAC began its experiments with microfranchising decades ago when it realized that merely lending to the poor would not be enough to lift them out of poverty. Dramatic improvement would come, however, with better access to markets, fairer prices, knowledge transfer and higher quality inputs like high-yield seeds and new breeds of chickens. BRAC created agricultural enterprises and services to enhance the business prospects of its microfinance borrowers and other members of poor communities. It used the same approach in providing health care, raising an army of "community health promoters" to provide simple but vital services in slums and villages, like de-worming medication and oral rehydration solution to treat diarrhea in young children.

Though largely unknown outside the international development community, experts have long noted the size and scope of BRAC's success in Bangladesh. Paul Collier, author of *The Bottom Billion*, has called BRAC "the most astounding social enterprise in the world." The *Economist* called it not only the largest but "one of the most businesslike" nongovernmental organizations in the world.

Today, BRAC is scaling up its microfranchising approach outside its native Bangladesh. Through a groundbreaking $45 million partnership with the MasterCard Foundation, BRAC has built a network of 3,500 microfranchised entrepreneurs in Uganda providing critical livelihood and health services to the poor. It currently operates in ten countries: Afghanistan, Bangladesh, Haiti, Liberia, Pakistan, Sierra Leone, South Sudan, Sri Lanka, Tanzania and Uganda.

About BRAC and the Microcredit Summit Campaign

BRAC, formerly the Bangladesh Rural Advancement Committee, is a global development organization dedicated to alleviating poverty by empowering the poor to bring about change in

The Difference Between Franchising and Microfranchising

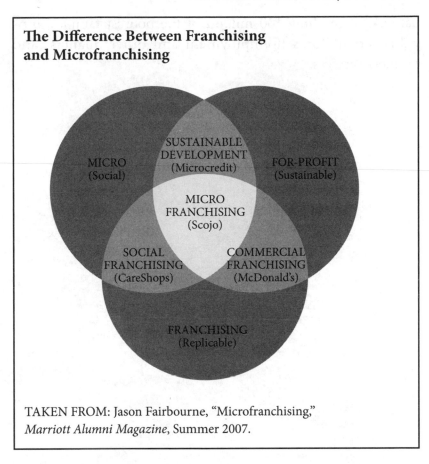

TAKEN FROM: Jason Fairbourne, "Microfranchising," *Marriott Alumni Magazine*, Summer 2007.

their own lives. BRAC's holistic approach aims to achieve large-scale, positive changes through economic and social programs that enable women and men to realize their potential. BRAC was launched in Bangladesh in 1972 and today reaches more than 138 million people in Africa and Asia through its programs that address poverty by providing microloans, self-employment opportunities, health services, education and legal and human rights services. . . .

The Microcredit Summit Campaign is a project of RESULTS Educational Fund, a U.S.-based advocacy organization committed to creating the will to eliminate poverty. The Campaign was launched in 1997 and, in 2007, surpassed its original goal of reaching 100 million of the poorest families, providing credit for self-employment and other financial and business services.

> *"The proliferation and democratization of technology has bested the economics of microenterprise."*

Microfranchising May Not Be a Solution to Global Poverty

Richard Shaffer

In the following viewpoint, Richard Shaffer contends that franchising intended to foster entrepreneurship in poverty-stricken countries, or microfranchising, may cease to be profitable as technology advances. Launched in 1997, a program in Bangladesh that enables the poor to buy and rent mobile phones was successful, he says, until mobile phones became more affordable and commonplace. Today, its participants do not earn enough to rise out of poverty, and a follow-up microfranchising program for Internet-service kiosks may be more difficult to implement, the author maintains. Based in New York, Shaffer is a writer covering technology and economics.

As you read, consider the following questions:

1. How does Laily Begum fare today in the mobile phone business, as described by Shaffer?

2. What is the shared access model, as explained by the author?

3. What is Shaffer's conclusion on the Village Phone Program?

At first, they all came. Not the beggars, of course, but villagers of every other sort, including many of the poorest. Most came in rickshaws, but some walked long distances across the rice paddies to line up at the door of a mud-walled home, waiting in the dust and the dung, with the chickens and the cows, even during Bangladesh's monsoon season, when the rain on the metal roof could make it difficult to hear.

And then, one by one, each talked on Laily Begum's wondrous new possession, a cellular telephone. A caller might come to check on money that her husband was supposed to send from his job as a day laborer in Dubai, or to keep tabs on the son who had moved to Chittagong in hopes of finding seaport work, or merely for gossip and the novelty of talking with someone far away.

But that was in the beginning, a decade ago; these days, cell phones are so commonplace that most visitors come only for a haircut, a shave, groceries, or a place to sleep, all of which Begum offers now. The few wireless calls are no longer made from her home but from one of her nearby shops—usually the one with the barrels, drums, and cans of motor oil out front and lining its walls. In March [2007], when I visited her home in Patira, a stretch of dusty intersections 90 minutes northeast of Dhaka, she told me, "Hardly anyone uses my phone anymore."

On March 26, 1997—chosen because that day was the anniversary of Bangladesh's independence from Pakistan—Begum became the first participant in Grameenphone's Village Phone Program. Now widely known, the plan offers small loans, or microcredit, that enable people in one of the world's most impoverished countries to buy cell phones and rent them, call by call, to neighbors who can't afford telephones of their own.

A compact, 44-year-old former seamstress with a skeptical look, Begum previously had borrowed and repaid lesser amounts to buy a cow, then another cow, and then to open a grocery store and tea shop for her husband. Next, she borrowed 25,000 takas, the equivalent at the time of about $580, to purchase her mobile telephone, a tall antenna, a heavy-duty battery, and some marketing materials. Almost immediately, she began earning more than that in monthly profits— approximately $800, or nearly twice as much in a month as the average Bangladeshi, even today, makes in an entire year.

A decade later, instead of begging on the streets and sleeping with cattle as she once had done, Begum shares a two-room brick house with her husband, two sons, a daughter, a television set, and a refrigerator. Next door, she has built a barn, shops, and temporary housing that she rents to five poor families. Today, her banker estimates her net worth at $145,000, which may be more than everyone else in her village combined.

Begum's success has become legendary, embraced by the media and the world of economic development as an example of how microcredit and technology can help those born in poverty escape it, largely through their own entrepreneurship. The Grameen organization continues to boast that its Village Phone Program "has been incredibly successful . . . establishing a clear path out of the poverty cycle" and in June published a manual, featuring a photograph of Begum, instructing microfinance lenders elsewhere how to follow its lead.

But as it turns out, the legend is far out of date. The proliferation and democratization of technology has bested the economics of microenterprise. In Bangladesh today, the only one making real money on Grameenphone's wireless service is . . . Grameenphone.

Making the Village Phone Obsolete

Grameenphone is a for-profit joint venture between Norway's Telenor and Grameen Telecom, a telecommunications affiliate of Grameen Bank, which won the Nobel Peace Prize last year [2006] together with its Bangladeshi founder, Muhammad Yunus. Grameenphone shares Grameen Bank's fundamental philosophy—that targeted loans of modest sums can be profitable and bring millions out of poverty. In fact, it has overcome risks—spending $1.2 billion, for example, on communications infrastructure in an impoverished land—that few others would have considered and has improved the lives of countless people.

All this has occurred in one of the most desperate nations on earth. Those of a certain age may remember [political scientist] Henry Kissinger's description of Bangladesh as a "bottomless basket," or [Beatles guitarist] George Harrison's all-star benefit concerts in the summer of 1971 as hundreds of thousands were dying in the war of independence from Pakistan. Usually, if we think of Bangladesh at all, we think of its poverty, violence, corruption, and disasters—its cyclones, droughts, and floods, its nationwide strikes, stalled traffic, militant bombings, pollution, erratic electricity, and beggars. Two out of every five Bangladeshis are officially classified as poor.

In aspiration and potential, however, Bangladesh is the Hong Kong of South Asia, with a resilient workforce, a growing middle class, and encouraging recent progress. The growth of real gross domestic product has increased to 6.7% last year from an annual average of 4.8% in the 1990s and 3.2% in the 1980s. Although the country's second-largest export continues to be its people—nearly 290,000 Bangladeshis work abroad, each sending home enough money to support 37 others—shipments of its principal manufactured exports, ready-made garments, have been rising 11% annually, despite recent loss of trade protection.

Grameen's Village Phone Program has mirrored that growth, expanding ten-thousand-fold in 10 years to include about 280,000 operators, mostly women known as "phone ladies." It has won fame because of its reputed earning power. "The typical village phone lady has an average income three times the national average," according to a 2005 United Nations manual explaining how to duplicate the program elsewhere. In the most recent book about the program, *You Can Hear Me Now*, published in February of this year, author Nicholas P. Sullivan writes, "It is widely accepted that village phone ladies can make anywhere from $750 to $1,200 a year."

The current reality, however, is something different. According to Grameen Telecom, the Grameenphone affiliate that manages the program, profits per operator have been declining for years and in 2006 averaged less than $70. "The program is not dead," says its manager, Mazharul Hannan, chief of technical services at Grameen Telecom, "but it is no longer a way out of poverty."

The reason is simple: Technology and Grameenphone itself have made the village phone obsolete. Access to cell phones has expanded rapidly across Bangladesh, as in other developing nations. Grameenphone, largest of the nation's six cellular providers, has more than 13 million subscribers, with yearly revenues of nearly $700 million. In all, perhaps one in seven Bangladeshis owns a phone, and ownership is expected to reach as high as one in three in a year or so.

Broadly Affordable

Ten years ago, Begum provided the sole telephone in Patira and the surrounding area, the only connection for nearly 10,000 people. Today, she must vie with 284 other Village Phone operators nearby, plus all the cell phones her neighbors have bought for themselves as prices have come down. As a result, Begum's phone rentals these days bring in monthly profits of only $22. "If I didn't have so many other businesses," she told me, "I couldn't afford to be in this one." Says her loan officer, Salim Khan, general manager of a Grameen Bank branch: "She is fortunate that she began when she did. Today, poor women who go into the phone business stay poor."

To understand the transformative power that cell phones have had in Bangladesh, one need only visit Dhaka, the capital. Dhaka is hot, humid, and flat, its skyline filled with cement buildings that seemingly aspire to East German monotony and dinginess. The city's air chokes with dust and the exhaust from ramshackle vehicles of every sort, patched together and resurfaced with fiberglass bonding compound, then gaily striped in turquoise, fuchsia, tangerine, chartreuse. Second globally only to Mumbai in the number of slum dwellers, the city is frenetic and noisy, with a constant beeping, honking, ringing, and coughing of buses, cars, rickshaws, and three-wheel taxis against the loud drone, in neighborhoods that can afford them, of electric generators. (Power fails several times a day.)

Yet across the city, cell phones are everywhere. In the Eastern Plaza, a multistory market building, several dozen cramped stalls offer phones exclusively. Because many handsets are smuggled into the country, suggested retail prices mean little, and bargaining is brisk.

Indeed, wireless has become broadly affordable—even in places that, until now, had no telephones of any sort. Advances in digital electronics have helped to lower the price of a cellular handset in poor nations from more than $400 to about $30. In practical terms, that's a reduction from more than the national average annual wage in those countries to less than the wages for a single month. As a result, many who once needed to use someone else's phone now can afford one of their own. . . .

A Shared Access Model

In the taxonomy of business, the Village Phone Program is a shared access model—a term that in the history of consumer technologies has included party lines, pay phones, Internet kiosks, radio receivers, television sets, and video-game consoles. Like those earlier products and services, its evolution has been, in hindsight, predictable: As innovations diffuse, ownership displaces rental.

In the 1980s, the government of India established "public call offices," small businesses that rented wired telephones to customers, call by call. "For about a decade, it was highly profitable," says Ashok Jhunjhunwala, a professor of electrical engineering at the Indian Institute of Technology Madras in Chennai, who has long studied the effects of computer and communications technologies on poverty. "But as more people got phones the profits disappeared."

Likewise, in the face of cheaper phones, accessible calling plans, and low-cost infrastructure, the phone ladies didn't stand a chance. Dawn Hartley, who manages the economic development fund of the GSM Association in London, a trade group that includes most wireless carriers, observes, "The outcome [for the Village Phone Program] was always inevitable. The shared access model is a halfway house between no one owning a mobile phone and everyone owning a mobile phone. Shared access models are a great bridge, and in some areas they will last a very long time, but by and large, they have a shelf life."

Not that the Village Phone Program is being abandoned. Indeed, it continues to recruit more operators. Although the program has become a marginal business for the typical phone lady, it may still contribute to Grameenphone's corporate net income—which is already robust. Despite peak rates that are among the world's lowest, less than two cents a minute, it earns operating margins of 42%.

That success reflects a radically different way of doing business, geared to the poor: efficient and low-cost carrier networking, billing, and customer-service systems and methods. "The efficiency involved in this makes or breaks a mobile service," Paul Budde, an authority on the telecommunications industry in South Asia, explained in an email. But it goes deeper than that. Grameen, for example, signs up most new customers these days without even supplying handsets. Vendors need only provide SIM [subscriber identity module] cards, the small, plastic memory circuitry that enables the network to identify a handset; where a customer gets the phone is his affair. And Grameen saves itself the cost of carrying all that phone inventory.

A Lever to Expand a Market

In much the same way, the Village Phone Program has served as a lever to efficiently expand Grameenphone's very lucrative market. Grameenphone's employees and managers also seem genuinely convinced of their duty to reduce poverty in Bangladesh. It is encouraging Village Phone operator-entrepreneurs to supplement incomes by selling SIM cards and over-the-air calling credits. In pilot projects, customers are paying utility bills over the phone and buying and selling goods via text messages. The company has provided more than 70,000 street beggars with interest-free loans, handsets, and wireless accounts, encouraging them to earn money by reselling airtime.

For now, Grameenphone is pinning most of its follow-on hopes on what it calls Community Information Centers, small kiosks—561 established already—in outlying villages that, for fees of 42 cents an hour, will offer such services as online browsing, agricultural and health care information, digital photography, video telephony via webcams, and electronic access to government reports and forms.

Such kiosks have met with little success in other countries, and Grameenphone concedes its plan is ambitious. "The business is similar to renting phones, but more difficult," said Mohammed Shafiqul Islam Sikdar, a deputy manager in the program. "With voice, the need was obvious; people want to talk to each other. With computer kiosks, it's not as clear what villagers will pay for and whether they will pay enough. Also, our entrepreneurs in this case have to be literate and have some technical skills. The capital requirements are greater, and as the sponsor, we're going to have to spend much more time and effort in marketing, support, and training. But we are in no hurry. We will make it work."

Meantime, Grameenphone is cooperating with nonprofits and other companies to expand the Village Phone Program beyond the borders of Bangladesh. Pilot programs are under way or being considered in Cambodia, Cameroon, Senegal, Mali, and the Democratic Republic of the Congo. The Grameen Foundation, on whose board Muhammad Yunus sits, has reproduced the program in Uganda and Rwanda, and is encouraging microfinance institutions elsewhere to clone more.

The effort is noble—and surely, the Village Phone Program has helped create a telecommunications infrastructure that supports economic development and greater prosperity for folks like Taiyeb Ali and Noor Alam. But the expansion effort is also disingenuous. In Grameen's promotional material for such programs, Yunus proclaims, "If a poor woman gets hold of one mobile phone in the village, then this is a sure bet that her entire family can move out of poverty in two or three years." In some indigent backwaters, that may still be true. But it's misleading, at best, to pretend that Bangladesh is among them.

Periodical and Internet Sources Bibliography

The following articles have been selected to supplement the diverse views presented in this chapter.

Carol C. Adelman and Nicholas Eberstadt
"Help That Helps," *Weekly Standard*, vol. 14, no. 46, August 31, 2009.

Mary Arnesen
"The Poverty Footprint," *Making It*, March 28, 2011. www.makingitmagazine.net.

Vikas Bajaj
"Sun Co-Founder Uses Capitalism to Help Poor," *New York Times*, October 5, 2010. www.nytimes.com.

Phyllis Bennis
"We Need Millennium Development Rights, Not Just Goals," *YES! Magazine*, September 27, 2010.

Thomas R. Eddlem
"The Toll of U.S. Foreign Aid," *New American*, March 7, 2011.

Justin Frewen
"Time to Revisit the Millennium Development Goals?," Worldpress.org, March 23, 2010. www.worldpress.org.

Bill Gates
"Making Capitalism More Creative," *Time*, July 31, 2008. www.time.com.

Joshua Kurlantzick
"The Death of Generosity," *Newsweek*, August 8, 2010.

Peter Newell
"Beyond CSR? Business, Poverty, and Social Justice," *Global Knowledge*, no. 2, 2008.

Lester M. Salamon
"Philanthropy's Blind Spot," *Alliance*, September 2011. www.alliancemagazine.org.

Victoria Schlesinger
"The Continuation of Poverty: Rebranding Foreign Aid in Kenya," *Harper's Magazine*, May 2007. http://harpers.org.

For Further Discussion

Chapter 1

1. David DeGraw criticizes the US Census Bureau for using outdated methods in determining national poverty statistics. As of September 2011, the bureau uses a new, updated poverty measure, but it does not replace the official poverty thresholds. In your view, does this reinforce DeGraw's criticism? Why or why not?

2. Robert Rector maintains that most poor Americans have a high standard of living. On the other hand, the Working Poor Families Project asserts that basic necessities are out of reach for many low-income citizens. In your opinion, who offers a more persuasive argument? Cite examples from the viewpoints to explain your response.

3. Joseph E. Stiglitz supports his position that the gap between rich and poor in the United States has grown by emphasizing the richest 1 percent of the population and their control over wealth. Terence Corcoran, however, examines the top 10 percent, insisting that incomes have remained flat for all but the richest 1 percent. In your opinion, does Corcoran successfully counter Stiglitz's argument? Cite examples from the texts to support your answer.

Chapter 2

1. Daniel Griswold contends that the migration of low-skilled immigrants to the United States may lower some wages but creates job opportunities for higher-skilled workers. In your view, does Griswold underplay the effect on wages he describes? Why or why not?

2. Steven Malanga suggests that people are poor through unwise personal decisions. In your opinion, is his assertion more compelling than the assertion of Claudia Rowe, who places blame on the recent recession and job loss? Use examples from the viewpoints to explain your response.

Chapter 3

1. Holly Sklar persists that the minimum wage does not adequately cover the costs of living, citing high rent costs and the numbers of employed people receiving food assistance. James Sherk, in contrast, proposes that most minimum-wage earners do not provide the main source of income in their households. In your view, who offers a stronger argument? Cite examples from the texts to support your answer.

2. Fred Goldstein alleges that welfare reform was designed to create a vast, low-wage workforce. Do you agree or disagree with Goldstein? Why or why not?

Chapter 4

1. J. Brian Atwood rejects the term "aid" in foreign aid, suggesting that it rewards poverty, creates dependency, and does not accurately describe "international development cooperation." Do you agree or disagree with the author? Use examples from the viewpoint to explain your response.

2. Peter Singer somewhat agrees with the claim that giving food or money to the poor creates dependency and supports this approach only for emergencies. In your view, does this undermine his plea for people to donate more? Why or why not?

Organizations to Contact

The editors have compiled the following list of organizations concerned with the issues debated in this book. The descriptions are derived from materials provided by the organizations. All have publications or information available for interested readers. The list was compiled on the date of publication of the present volume; the information provided here may change. Be aware that many organizations take several weeks or longer to respond to inquiries, so allow as much time as possible.

American Enterprise Institute for Public Policy Research (AEI)
1150 Seventeenth Street NW, Washington, DC 20036
(202) 862-5800 • fax: (202) 862-7177
e-mail: webmaster@aei.org
website: www.aei.org

The American Enterprise Institute for Public Policy Research (AEI) is an independent, nonprofit research organization associated with the neoconservative movement in American politics. AEI scholars advocate limited government, tax reduction, capitalist enterprise, and individual responsibility as the best responses to poverty. AEI's website offers an archive of op-eds, newsletters, position papers, government testimony, and longer monographs on poverty-related topics such as welfare and health insurance reform, as well as the daily online business magazine the *American*.

Benefits.gov
(800) FED-INFO (333-4636)
website: www.benefits.gov

Sponsored by a partnership of federal agencies including all cabinet-level departments, the Social Security Administration, and the US Small Business Administration, Benefits.gov is the official benefits website of the US government, with the most comprehensive and up-to-date information on more than one thousand federal and state benefits and assistance programs for poor Americans. Searchable by state, the site explains eligibility requirements and provides links for food/nutrition (such as food stamps and WIC), education, housing, health care, and job-training programs.

Brookings Institution
1775 Massachusetts Avenue NW, Washington, DC   20036
(202) 797-6000 • fax: (202) 797-6004
e-mail: brookinfo@brook.edu
website: www.brookings.edue

Brookings Institution, founded in 1927, is a liberal-centrist think tank whose fellows conduct research on and debate issues of foreign policy, economics, government, and the social sciences. Its scholars publish analyses of domestic and global antipoverty policy in the quarterly journal *Brookings Review* and in position papers such as "Immigration and Poverty in America's Suburbs" and "Fighting Poverty the American Way."

Cato Institute
1000 Massachusetts Avenue NW
Washington, DC   20001-5403
(202) 842-0200 • fax: (202) 842-3490
website: www.cato.org

Cato Institute is a libertarian public policy research foundation dedicated to individual liberty, free markets, and limited government. It opposes minimum wage laws, trade barriers, and expansion of executive power; it supports non-interventionist foreign policy, a balanced federal budget, and workers' rights to opt out of the Social Security program. It offers numerous publications on public policy, including the triannual *Cato Journal*, the bimonthly newsletter *Cato Policy Report*, and the quarterly magazine *Regulation*. Numerous poverty-related studies and position papers are available on the website.

Center on Budget and Policy Priorities (CBPP)

820 First Street NE, Suite 510, Washington, DC   20002
(202) 408-1080 • fax: (202) 408-1056
e-mail: center@cbpp.org
website: www.cbpp.org

The Center on Budget and Policy Priorities (CBPP) is a non-profit research and advocacy group that researches and represents the needs of low-income people in setting budget and tax policy. Founded in 1981 to analyze federal budget priorities, CBPP expanded its focus in the 1990s to funding for the poor at the state level (the State Fiscal Analysis Initiative) and in developing countries (the International Budget Project). The center maintains an online library of reports, statistics, slide shows, and analyses of the government's poverty and income data.

Children's Defense Fund (CDF)

25 E Street NW, Washington, DC   20001
(800) 233-1200
e-mail: cdfinfo@childrensdefense.org
website: www.childrensdefense.org

Children's Defense Fund (CDF), founded in 1973, is a private, nonprofit organization that aims to ensure the health, education, and safety of all children. Led by founder and president Marian Wright Edelman, the fund lobbies legislators in support of Medicaid and the Children's Health Insurance Program (CHIP), the Head Start early education program, and other services for disadvantaged and poor children. Numerous publications are available for free download from the fund's website, including "A Portrait of Inequality" and fact sheets by state on child poverty, hunger, welfare, health, education, and at-risk youth.

Coalition on Human Needs (CHN)

1120 Connecticut Avenue NW, Suite 312
Washington, DC   20036
(202) 223-2532 • fax: (202) 223-2538

e-mail: info@chn.org
website: www.chn.org

Coalition on Human Needs (CHN) is an alliance of national organizations working together to promote public policies that address the needs of low-income and other vulnerable people. The coalition promotes adequate funding for human needs programs, progressive tax policies, and other federal measures to address the needs of low-income and other vulnerable populations. It publishes the *Human Needs Report* newsletter every other Friday when Congress is in session.

Economic Policy Institute (EPI)

1333 H Street NW, Suite 300, East Tower
Washington, DC 20005-4707
(202) 775-8810 • fax: (202) 775-0819
e-mail: epi@epi.org
website: www.epi.org

Economic Policy Institute (EPI) is a nonprofit, progressive think tank created in 1986 to represent the interests of low- and middle-income workers in the debate over US economic policy. It supports minimum-wage laws and workers' rights to form unions. Its fellows track trends in wages, benefits, union participation, and other economic indicators; testify before Congress and state legislatures; advise policy makers; and publish books, studies, and issue guides on poverty-related topics such as welfare, offshoring, and the living wage. EPI also produces the biennial *The State of Working America* and commentaries and reports.

Grameen Bank

Mirpur-2, Dhaka-1216
Bangladesh
(880-2) 8011138 • fax: (880-2) 8013559
e-mail: grameen.bank@grameen.net
website: www.grameen-info.org

Winner of the 2006 Nobel Peace Prize, Grameen Bank is an example of the microcredit, or microfinance, approach to reducing global poverty—issuing collateral-free loans to the poor to establish small businesses at the village level. Founded by Bangladeshi economist Muhammad Yunus in 1976, Grameen is 94 percent owned by and works exclusively for its borrowers, 97 percent of whom are women. The bank's website includes FAQs and explanations of initiatives and is a source for understanding how microfinance works in the developing world.

Heritage Foundation

214 Massachusetts Avenue NE, Washington, DC   20002
(202) 546-4400 • fax: (202) 546-0904
e-mail: info@heritage.org
website: www.heritage.org

The Heritage Foundation is a conservative, public policy research institute dedicated to "principles of free enterprise, limited government, individual freedom, traditional American values, and a strong national defense." Its resident scholars publish position papers on a wide range of complex issues in its *Backgrounder* series and in its quarterly journal, *Policy Review*. Numerous poverty-related documents are archived on the foundation's website, which also offers commentaries, podcasts, and a blog.

United Nations Development Programme (UNDP)

One United Nations Plaza, New York, NY   10017
(212) 906-5000
website: www.undp.org

In January 2007, the United Nations' Millennium Project—eight global development goals adopted by 189 nations in 2000—was folded into the United Nations Development Programme (UNDP), the UN network that helps governments address development problems such as democratic governance, poverty reduction, crisis prevention and recovery, energy and environment use, and HIV/AIDS. Resources can be found in the site's Millennium Development Goals and Poverty Reduction sections, which explain and track in detail worldwide efforts to achieve Millennium Goal 1 (MDG1), the commitment to cut global poverty in half by 2015.

US Census Bureau
4600 Silver Hill Road, Washington, DC   20233
(301) 763-4636
e-mail: pop@census.gov
website: www.census.gov

The US Census Bureau is responsible for the US census, which is the official source of statistics on poverty in America. Its website includes sections about how poverty is measured, definitions of poverty-related terms, up-to-date dollar amounts used to determine poverty status, poverty causes and projections, comparisons with poverty in foreign countries, and common questions and answers. Numerous reports and briefs available for download include the annual *Income, Poverty, and Health Insurance Coverage in the United States* and *The Effects of Taxes and Transfers on Income and Poverty in the United States.*

World Bank
1818 H Street NW, Washington, DC   20433
(202) 473-1000 • fax: (202) 477-6391
website: www.worldbank.org

World Bank comprises two institutions owned by 187 member countries: the International Bank for Reconstruction and Development (IBRD) and the International Development Association (IDA). World Bank offers poverty assessments of countries in which it has an active program, working with national institutions, development agencies, and other organizations. Data on its website includes measures of the population living below the national and international poverty lines. Other information, such as urban and rural poverty rates and income distributions, is also presented.

Bibliography of Books

Abhijit V.
Banerjee and
Esther Duflo

Poor Economics: A Radical Rethinking of the Way to Fight Global Poverty. New York: PublicAffairs, 2011.

Matthew Bishop
and Michael
Green

Philanthrocapitalism: How the Rich Can Save the World. New York: Bloomsbury Press, 2008.

Paul Collier

The Bottom Billion: Why the Poorest Countries Are Failing and What Can Be Done About It. New York: Oxford University Press, 2007.

Daryl Collins,
Jonathan
Morduch, Stuart
Rutherford, and
Orlanda Ruthven

Portfolios of the Poor: How the World's Poor Live on $2 a Day. Princeton, NJ: Princeton University Press, 2009.

Jane L. Collins
and Victoria
Mayer

Both Hands Tied: Welfare Reform and the Race to the Bottom in the Low-Wage Labor Market. Chicago, IL: University of Chicago Press, 2010.

Steve Corbett and
Brian Fikkert

When Helping Hurts: How to Alleviate Poverty Without Hurting the Poor . . . and Yourself. Chicago, IL: Moody Publishers, 2009.

Arjan de Haan

How the Aid Industry Works: An Introduction to International Development. Sterling, VA: Kumarian Press, 2009.

Kathryn Edin and
Maria Kefalas
Promises I Can Keep: Why Poor Women Put Motherhood Before Marriage. Berkeley: University of California Press, 2005.

Barbara
Ehrenreich
Nickel and Dimed: On (Not) Getting By in America. New York: Holt Paperbacks, 2008.

Steven H.
Goldberg
Billions of Drops in Millions of Buckets: Why Philanthropy Doesn't Advance Social Progress. Hoboken, NJ: John Wiley & Sons, 2009.

R. Glenn
Hubbard and
William Duggan
The Aid Trap: Hard Truths About Ending Poverty. New York: Columbia Business School Publishing, 2009.

Dean Karlan and
Jacob Appel
More than Good Intentions: How a New Economics Is Helping to Solve Global Poverty. New York: Dutton, 2011.

Anirudh Krishna
One Illness Away: Why People Become Poor and How They Escape Poverty. New York: Oxford University Press, 2010.

Sandra Morgen,
Joan Acker, and
Jill Weigt
Stretched Thin: Poor Families, Welfare Work, and Welfare Reform. Ithaca, NY: Cornell University Press, 2010.

Dambisa Moyo
Dead Aid: Why Aid Is Not Working and How There Is a Better Way for Africa. New York: Farrar, Straus and Giroux, 2009.

Katherine S. Newman and Rourke O'Brien	*Taxing the Poor: Doing Damage to the Truly Disadvantaged.* Berkeley: University of California Press, 2011.
Paul Polak	*Out of Poverty: What Works When Traditional Approaches Fail.* San Francisco, CA: Berrett-Koehler Publishers, 2008.
Robert Pollin, Mark Brenner, Jeannette Wicks-Lim, and Stephanie Luce	*A Measure of Fairness: The Economics of Living Wages and Minimum Wages in the United States.* Ithaca, NY: Cornell University Press, 2008.
Roger C. Riddell	*Does Foreign Aid Really Work?* New York: Oxford University Press, 2007.
Paul Ryscavage	*Rethinking the Income Gap: The Second Middle Class Revolution.* New Brunswick, NJ: Transaction Publishers, 2009.
Bradley R. Schiller	*The Economics of Poverty and Discrimination.* Upper Saddle River, NJ: Pearson/Prentice Hall, 2008.
Sudhir Alladi Venkatesh	*Off the Books: The Underground Economy of the Urban Poor.* Cambridge, MA: Harvard University Press, 2006.
William Voegeli	*Never Enough: America's Limitless Welfare State.* New York: Encounter Books, 2010.
William Julius Wilson	*More than Just Race: Being Black and Poor in the Inner City.* New York: W.W. Norton & Company, 2009.

Muhammad
Yunus

Creating a World Without Poverty: Social Business and the Future of Capitalism. New York: PublicAffairs, 2009.

Index

R